Inspiring Thoughts to Jump-Start Your Day

Volume 2

Simeon Rosete, Jr., D.B.S.

TEACH Services, Inc.
PUBLISHING
www.TEACHServices.com • (800) 367-1844

World rights reserved. This book or any portion thereof may not be copied or reproduced in any form or manner whatever, except as provided by law, without the written permission of the publisher, except by a reviewer who may quote brief passages in a review.

The author assumes full responsibility for the accuracy of all facts and quotations as cited in this book. The opinions expressed in this book are the author's personal views and interpretations, and do not necessarily reflect those of the publisher.

This book is provided with the understanding that the publisher is not engaged in giving spiritual, legal, medical, or other professional advice. If authoritative advice is needed, the reader should seek the counsel of a competent professional.

Copyright © 2020 Simeon Rosete, Jr., D.B.S.
Copyright © 2020 TEACH Services, Inc.
ISBN-13: 978-1-4796-1152-2 (Paperback)
ISBN-13: 978-1-4796-1153-9 (ePub)
Library of Congress Control Number: 2020905746

All scripture quotations, unless otherwise indicated, are taken from the KING JAMES VERSION (KJV): KING JAMES VERSION, public domain.

Scripture quotations marked NKJV are taken from the NEW KING JAMES VERSION (NKJV): Scripture taken from the NEW KING JAMES VERSION®. Copyright © 1982 by Thomas Nelson, Inc. Used by permission. All rights reserved.

Scripture quotations marked NHEB are taken from the New Heart English Bible. This version is not copyrighted and is dedicated to the Public Domain by the editors and translators.

Scriptures quotations marked ESV are taken from THE HOLY BIBLE, ENGLISH STANDARD VERSION (ESV): Scriptures taken from THE HOLY BIBLE, ENGLISH STANDARD VERSION ® Copyright© 2001 by Crossway, a publishing ministry of Good News Publishers. Used by permission.

Scripture quotations marked NLT are taken from the HOLY BIBLE, NEW LIVING TRANSLATION (NLT): Scriptures taken from the HOLY BIBLE, NEW LIVING TRANSLATION, Copyright© 1996, 2004, 2007 by Tyndale House Foundation. Used by permission of Tyndale House Publishers, Inc., Carol Stream, Illinois 60188. All rights reserved. Used by permission.

Scripture quotations marked TM are taken from THE MESSAGE: THE BIBLE IN CONTEMPORARY ENGLISH (TM): Scripture taken from THE MESSAGE: THE BIBLE IN CONTEMPORARY ENGLISH, copyright© 1993, 1994, 1995, 1996, 2000, 2001, 2002. Used by permission of NavPress Publishing Group.

Scripture quotations marked NAS are taken from the NEW AMERICAN STANDARD (NAS): Scripture taken from the NEW AMERICAN STANDARD BIBLE®, copyright© 1960, 1962, 1963, 1968, 1971, 1972, 1973, 1975, 1977, 1995 by The Lockman Foundation. Used by permission.

The website references in this book have been shortened using a URL shortener and redirect service called 1ref.us, which TEACH Services manages. If you find that a reference no longer works, please contact us and let us know which one is not working so that we can correct it. Any personal website addresses that the author included are managed by the author. TEACH Services is not responsible for the accuracy or permanency of any links.

Dedication

To Ellen Pacheco Rosete, the beautiful love of my life, who has been my faithful and steady partner through all forty-seven years of my ministry.

Table of Contents

Acknowledgements 11
Introduction 13
Beauty Tips 14
Thank God, We Are Free! 15
Another Year for Him 17
Our Greatest and Most Urgent Need 18
Eagles in a Storm 19
Jesus Gave His All 20
The Carpenter 21
Obstacles in Our Path 23
Beyond the Cross 24
On Sand and in Stone 25
If You Know the Secret, Pass It On 26
The Cross 28
God Is a Refuge in Time of Trouble 29
It Matters Where You Look 30
Judging Gently 32
Christ Our Only Hope 33
A Lesson in Philosophy 34
"Night Watch" 36
"Be Still and Know..." 38
The Power of Being 39
To Judge or Not to Judge 40
That Personal Touch 41
Total Surrender 42
Valleys Don't Last Forever 43
"A Woman and a Fork" 44
"The Brick" 46
Growth Time in the Valley 48
Love Finds a Way 50
How to be Happy 51
Put Down Your Burdens 53

Twice Owned 54
Ways to Reduce Stress in Our Lives 56
Do You Know Yourself? 59
The Tater People 60
Making a Difference 62
The Need to Be Positive 64
In the Cross of Christ 65
Advice for a Happy Life 67
God's Ways Are Best 69
God's Hand 70
An Intercontinental Journey 72
Just a Little More 74
This Too Shall Pass 75
A Journey Through Life 77
Helpful Hints for Relaxation in the Lord 80
Shipwrecked 82
Heaven—Who Will Be There? 83
When Doors Close 84
The Ministry of Trials 85
"My Word...Shall Not Return to Me Void" (Isa. 55:11) 87
The King Who Was Obedient 89
Blessings Missed 90
Rust Out or Wear Out? 92
Worshiping God or Flattering the King? 93
Trees in the Summer Heat 94
Ten Signs That Show You Could Live to Be a Hundred 96
The Ant and the Leaf 99
The Greatest Hazard in Life 101
The Mountain Man 102
The Master's Touch 104
The Woodcutter 106
Things Closest to Us 108
Just Trust His Heart 109

When It's Time to Change Your Life 110
When Life Breaks Down 112
Why I Stay Away from Church 113
Hands Uplifted for an Open Mind 115
Contented or Covetous? 116
Most Dangerous Times for the Heart 117
Diet, Fatigue, and Sleeping Difficulties 119
The Fight Against Alzheimer's Disease 120
Grandparenting to Sharpen the Mind 122
Honoring Grandparents 123
Hurried and Busy or Composed and Relaxed? 124
Rocks, Rocks, and More Rocks 125
Khrushchev and the Bible 126
Kill the Church or Care for It? 127
The Beggar Who Was King 129
Loving Ourselves 130
Making the Devil Flee 131
Tribute to Mothers 132
Men and Women the World Needs Today 134
The Battle is the Lord's 135
God Never Makes Mistakes 137
The Agony of Defeat 139
Carelessness in Little Things 141
"Greater is He That Is in You" 142
Hope in the Land of Captivity 143
Do We See the Little Bandaged Fingers? 145
One Dark Night in Las Vegas 146
A Letter to Dads 148
A Time for Celebration? 150
A Tragedy or a Blessing? 152
Let Them Hear It Now 154
Built on a Rock 155
Backward, Christian Soldiers! 157

The Da Vinci Code	159
Making Sense of the World	160
Cell Phones Versus the Bible	161
The Twenty-Third Psalm	162
Signs of Spiritual Awakening	164
"No Time for God?"	165
Aging Gracefully	166
Twenty-Six Guards	168
Living to Bless Others	170
Some Valuable Quotes	172
People Need the Lord	173
Things I Wish I Had Known Before I Was Twenty-One	174
Running .... and Finishing the Race	175
The Little Things	176
Every Day Is Special	177
You Are Special	178
Is God Real to You?	180
Christians and Pumpkins	181
What Church Are You Looking For?	182
A New Way of Tithing	183
Prescription for Unhappiness	184
How to Be Perfectly Miserable	186
Becoming a Friend and Staying That Way	188
Lessons from the Butterfly	189
Six Things to Give	190
Where God Is	191
I Was a Stranger	192
The Serenity Prayer	193
The Way Up Is the Way Out	194
Living in Relationships	195
The Rope	196
"God, Speak to Me!"	197
The Spider Web	198

Happy People 1	200
Happy People 2	201
Best Places to Live in the World	203
I Wish You Enough	204
God Has Paid It All	206
The Power and Patience of Love	208
You Are Blessed	209
"Mister, Are You Jesus?"	210
How to Stay Young	212
Life	215
A Different Kind of Prayer	217
Making Time for the Things That Really Count	219
Would You Run?	220
Life Is a Matter of Priorities	221
The Parable of the Pencil	223
Sharing in the Joys of Creation	224
Moments with God	225
God Elected You	226
A Red-Letter Day in History	227
The Golden Box	229
The Passion of the Christ	230
Secrets of a Happy Life	231
The Day God Visited	232
A Prayer	234
Happy Thanksgiving, Everyone!	236
Reverse or Proper Proportion of Thanksgiving?	237
Why the Nine Did Not Return	238
Giving Thanks	240
If You Never	241
Thank You, Lord	243
When to Say "Thank You" to God	245
Happiness is Now	247
Be Thankful, Always	248

Happy Thanksgiving Day to All!	250
The Shipwreck	251
The Ant and the Contact Lens	252
Are You Saving for Eternity?	253
Getting Bold for Christ	255
God Has a Need for You	256
Scenic Wonders of Scandinavia and Russia	257
Christmastime	259
The Colors of Christmas	260
Christmas Is About Leaving Home	262
Finding Christ and Worshiping Him This Christmas	263
Looking for Christ at Christmas	265
A Heads Up for Christmas Gift-givers	267
What Would You Have Done?	269
All I Want for Christmas	270
The Christmas Story in Modern Version	272
A Time for Sharing	273
God Is Like…	274
Special Gifts this Season	276
The Night Before Christmas	278
As We Celebrate Christmas	279
Why Jesus is the Reason for the Season	280
What Kind of Church Are We?	281
Marks of Revival	283
Communion—A Time for Rededication	284
Are You Faithful?	285
Lose Weight by Turning the TV Off	286
Just Suppose	287
It Has Been a Good Year, Thank God	288
Resolutions for the New Year	289
New Year's Resolutions	291
About the Author	293
Endnotes	295

Acknowledgements

I want to express my appreciation to the members of the Central Filipino Church of Seventh-day Adventists, in Los Angeles, California, who called me from my ministerial work in the Philippines to come and serve them as their senior pastor. They have been an encouragement and support to my ministry through the twenty-five years that I have been with them to the present day. It was to them that these messages were initially directed.

My thanks go especially to Dr. Alfonso Miguel, Jr., and Rey Regoso, head elder and associate head elder, respectively.

My gratitude goes to Dianne Fabrigar Cruz for her computer skills in retrieving the files of these messages from the church office for so many years during her tenure as church office secretary.

I also want to thank my family for the support they gave to this project. My wife, Ellen, has allowed me to take time to write. I also thank my children (Joenilyn and her husband Wilfredo Navarro, Jr.; Jocelyn; Samuel; Jane and her husband Carlo Verde) and my grandchildren (Katelynn, Ariana, Ella, and Cruz) for being such an inspiration during the creation of these messages.

Introduction

The materials in this volume are messages that I placed in my church's weekly bulletin as an encouragement to the members of my congregation through the years. In addition to the weekly sermon, I thought it best to give members a short devotional thought that they could take home with them following the church service—a thought on which they could meditate during the following week and through the rest of their lives.

This volume, then, is a compilation of my experiences and thoughts as I pastored my flock, together with a host of materials that I gathered from a variety of sources through the years. It didn't take long before I learned that my congregation was being richly blessed by these messages and that they were filing them for future reference. Some of them mentioned how these became a convenient source of short, inspirational messages that they themselves delivered when the occasion arose.

Then an idea came from a number of these friends: they asked me if I could publish these messages in book form and circulate it as widely as possible, so that many more people could be blessed. That is how this book came to be.

Needless to say, the materials have been edited and appear in a slightly different format from the original to make them better suited to this book. But a number of the messages still retain characteristics of the narrative related to the experiences of my life and ministry for my congregation.

I trust that you will find these messages to be uplifting and truly devotional, in a way that will jump-start your day and help make each day of your life worth living!

Beauty Tips

Everyone wants to be beautiful. Some go to great lengths and tremendous expense just to improve their looks and make themselves attractive. But physical beauty is relative, and it oftentimes rests in the eye of the beholder. The real kind of beauty is not skin-deep. A really beautiful person is beautiful through and through.

Sam Levenson suggests ways to achieve this kind of beauty. Although his advice is directed to women as they are often the ones obsessed with trying to be beautiful, these suggestions apply to men as well.

"For attractive lips, speak words of kindness. For lovely eyes, seek out the good in people. For a slim figure, share your food with the hungry. For beautiful hair, let a child run his fingers through it once a day. For poise, walk with the knowledge you'll never walk alone."[1]

"The beauty of a woman is not in the clothes she wears,
the figure that she carries, or the way she combs her hair.
The beauty of a woman is seen in her eyes, because that is the
doorway to her heart, the place where love resides."[2]

"The beauty of a woman is not in a facial mole,
but true beauty in a woman is reflected in her soul.
It is the caring that she lovingly gives,
the passion that she knows."[3]

"And the beauty of a woman,
with passing years only grows!"[4]

Thank God, We Are Free!

Every July, America celebrates its independence as a nation. The Stars and Stripes is proudly hoisted from homes, offices, and cars, symbolizing people's gratitude to God for this beautiful land that is America. It is also a way of paying tribute to the founding fathers and the heroes who sacrificed and shed their blood so that generations to come (and all those who will set foot on its shores) will have the freedom to enjoy life and all its blessings. Just as displaying the Stars and Stripes symbolizes our gratitude to God for the beautiful land that is America, so our resting on the Sabbath symbolizes our freedom that Jesus gives us from the burden of sin and guilt.

In the beginning, when God created this beautiful world, He gave the Sabbath to man as a memorial of His creative work. He also instituted this day for man to have a day of rest and be able to worship his Creator. And when this world was lost through man's fall and Satan took dominion over it, Jesus came to die on the cross so that He could redeem this world. All those who accept Him as Lord and Savior may once again have the freedom to live lives of happiness and peace here in this world—and in the new earth for all eternity. In a special sense, the Sabbath is also a symbol of the rest that man may experience from the burden of sin and guilt for all eternity.

The question for all of us is: are we enjoying the freedom that Jesus came to purchase so dearly with His blood? He declares "And you shall know the truth, and the truth shall make you free" (John 8:32, NKJV).

The truth is God's Word. He says, "Sanctify them through thy truth, thy Word is truth" (John 17:17). And more than that, the truth is a person.

In fact, that person is Jesus Christ Himself. His Word says "…I am the way, the truth, and the life…" (John 14:6).

When we come to know and accept Him who is truth, we will have freedom all our lives—here and for all eternal ages.

Another Year for Him

Whatever disappointments or failures we had in the past year are past. They are done, and there is nothing more we can do about them—except to bury them in oblivion, nevermore to be reminded of them, except to make sure they never happen again.

Now God in His mercy has given us another chance. This New Year comes to us like a book with blank pages. It depends on us how it will look by year's end. Will it be a duplicate of the previous year with its blemishes and spots? Or will it be an updated, revised version with new territories acquired and new heights attained?

By the end of the year, we will know that we have succeeded if we have lived for the Lord and put service to others as more important than service to ourselves.

A poem written by Frances Ridley Havergal (1836–1879), entitled "Another Year is Dawning," bears consideration.

> Another year is dawning, dear Father, let it be
> In working, or in waiting, another year with Thee.
> Another year of progress, another year of praise,
> Another year of proving Thy presence all the days.
> Another year of mercies, of faithfulness and grace,
> Another year of gladness in the shining of Thy face…
> Another year of service, of witness for Thy love,
> Another year of training for holier work above.
> Another year is dawning, dear Father, let it be
> On earth, or else in Heaven, another year for Thee."[5]

May we all find success this year by living for the Lord and serving our fellow man.

Our Greatest and Most Urgent Need

We are now living in the last days of this earth's history, and it is about time to focus our minds on things of eternity, with an awareness that nothing else really matters. Let us pray earnestly for this, knowing that no genuine revival ever happened in the history of the church without much prayer and searching of the heart.

Ellen G. White says that our greatest and most urgent need is the revival of true and primitive godliness among us.[6] This can only be done through the gift of the Holy Spirit. We have a work cut out for us, and this work can be done—not by our churches becoming filled with men and women, but by men and women becoming filled with God.

We don't have to work hard for revival and reformation to happen. All we need to do is to cease our striving, "Be still and know" that He is God (Psalm 46:10), and let Him do His will in us.

As G. Campbell Morgan says, "Revival cannot be organized, but we can set our sails to catch the wind from heaven when God chooses to blow upon His people once again."[7]

Robert Coleman says that, when revival happens, God "visits his own people, restoring…and releasing them into the fullness of his blessing."[8]

Let us pray for a revival in our lives and in the life of the church. As we bare our souls and await the infilling of the Holy Spirit, let us get ready for God's visitation upon us, restoring our souls and releasing us into the fullness of His blessing.

Eagles in a Storm

We are told that "an eagle knows when a storm is approaching long before it breaks. The eagle will fly to some high spot and wait for the winds to come. When the storm hits, it sets its wings so that the wind picks it up and lifts it above the storm. While the storm rages below, the eagle is soaring above it. The eagle does not escape the storm. It simply uses the storm to lift it higher. It rises on the winds that bring the storm."[9] Wait on God. He will help us soar as an eagle about the storms of life.

We can learn from the eagle. Failure, disappointment, tragedy, illness, and other misfortunes may come upon us. When these storms of life occur, let us rise above them by riding on the winds. We can do this by setting our minds on God. The storms won't overcome us because we will be above them. God's power will lift us up, and we can soar to the heights of the Spirit.

> *Wait on God. He will help us soar as an eagle about the storms of life.*

Let us wait on God. He enables us to ride the winds of the storm in our lives. We can soar like the eagle. The prophet Isaiah says, "But they that wait on the Lord shall renew their strength; they shall mount up with wings like eagles; they shall run, and not be weary; and they shall walk, and not faint" (Isa. 40:31).

Jesus Gave His All

A chaplain was visiting a soldier, who was lying on a cot in a hospital. "You have lost an arm in the great cause," he said.

"No," said the soldier with a smile. "I didn't lose it–I gave it."

In the same way, Jesus did not lose His life—He gave it on purpose. He said, "Therefore My Father loves Me, because I lay down My life that I may take it again. No one takes it from Me, but I lay it down of Myself. I have power to lay it down, and I have power to take it again" (John 10:17–18, NKJV).

And Jesus gave His life because of His love for us. He wants us to live with Him forever. All we need to do is accept His love and love Him and then live for Him in return.

So let us give Him our best, as we serve Him for the rest of our lives.

The Carpenter

Once upon a time,[10] two brothers, who lived on adjoining farms, fell into conflict. It was the first serious rift in forty years of farming side-by-side, sharing machinery, and trading labor and goods as needed—all without a hitch.

Then the long collaboration fell apart. It began with a small misunderstanding, and it grew into a major difference. Finally, it exploded into an exchange of bitter words followed by weeks of silence.

One morning there was a knock on the older brother's door. He opened it to find a man carrying a carpenter's toolbox.

"I'm looking for a few days' work," he said. "Perhaps you have a few small jobs here and there that I could do. Could I help you?"

"Yes," said the older brother. "I do have a job for you. Look across the creek at that farm. That's my neighbor. In fact, he's my younger brother! Last week there was a meadow between us. He recently took his bulldozer to the river levee and now there is a creek between us. Well, he may have done this to spite me, but I'll do him one better. See that pile of lumber by the barn? I want you to build me a fence, an 8-foot fence—so I won't need to see his place or his face anymore."

The carpenter said, "I think I understand the situation. Show me the nails and the posthole digger, and I'll be able to do a job that pleases you."

The older brother had to go to town, so he helped the carpenter get the materials ready, and then he was off for the day. The carpenter worked hard all that day—measuring, sawing, and nailing.

It was about sunset when the older brother returned, and the carpenter had just finished his job. The older brother's eyes opened wide, and his jaw dropped. There was no fence there at all. It was a bridge— a bridge that stretched from one side of the creek to the other! A fine piece of work, handrails and all! And the neighbor, his younger brother, was coming toward them, his hand outstretched!

"You are quite a fellow to build this bridge after all I've said and done," the younger brother said to his older brother.

The two brothers stood at each end of the bridge, and then they met in the middle, taking each other's hand. They turned to see the carpenter hoist his toolbox onto his shoulder.

"No, wait! Stay a few days. I have a lot of other projects for you," said the older brother.

"I'd love to stay on," the carpenter said, "but I have many more bridges to build."

How much better this world would be if we went around every day just like the carpenter, looking for work to do—not erecting fences or barricades, but putting up bridges to span chasms of hatred, prejudice, and indifference. Surely, our homes, our schools, our church's, and this world would be a more peaceful and much better place to live in while we wait and help prepare people for the soon return of Jesus Christ.

Jesus Himself said, "Blessed are the peacemakers: for they shall be called the children of God" (Matt. 5:9).

Obstacles in Our Path

"In ancient times, a King had a boulder placed on a roadway. Then he hid himself and watched to see if anyone would remove the huge rock. Some of the king's wealthiest merchants and courtiers came by and simply walked around it. Many loudly blamed the King for not keeping the roads clear, but none did anything about getting the stone out of the way.

Then a peasant came along carrying a load of vegetables. Upon approaching the boulder, the peasant laid down his burden and tried to move the stone to the side of the road. After much pushing and straining, he finally succeeded.

After the peasant picked up his load of vegetables, he noticed a purse lying in the road where the boulder had been. The purse contained many gold coins and a note from the King indicating that the gold was for the person who removed the boulder from the roadway.

The peasant learned what many others never understand:

'Every obstacle presents an opportunity to improve one's condition.'"[11]

As we face the obstacles that life presents to us, let us realize the opportunities that come with them. Let us use them—not only to make our world a better place to live in, but also as a way to improve ourselves and make our situation better. So let us keep our eyes open and accept every obstacle and trial as coming from God to test us, to develop our patience, and, finally, to make us perfect in Him.

The apostle James says: "My brethren, count it all joy when ye fall into divers temptations; knowing this, that the trying of your faith worketh patience. But let patience have her perfect work, that ye may be perfect and entire, wanting nothing" (James 1:2–4).

Beyond the Cross

"Every year, people climb a mountain in the Italian Alps and stand at an outdoor crucifix.... A tourist noticed that a little trail led [beyond the cross]. He made his way down the trail, and, to his surprise, he found another shrine overgrown with brush. This shrine symbolized the empty tomb. Unfortunately, it had been neglected."[12] Almost everyone had gone as far as the cross, but there they stopped.

So many go to the cross to be able to experience the despair and heartbreak associated with it. Very few have moved beyond the cross to be able to discover the empty tomb. That is the message of the resurrection.

In our spiritual journey, let us find both the cross and the empty tomb. Let us realize that Christ died on the cross for our sins, but that He is also risen and alive forevermore. And because He is alive, we, too, shall be made alive if we die in Him.

1 Corinthians 15:14-22 says:

"And if Christ be not risen, then is our preaching vain, and your faith is also vain.

Yea, and we are found false witnesses of God; because we have testified of God that he raised up Christ: whom he raised not up, if so be that the dead rise not.

For if the dead rise not, then is not Christ raised:

And if Christ be not raised, your faith is vain; ye are yet in your sins.

Then they also which are fallen asleep in Christ are perished. If in this life only we have hope in Christ, we are of all men most miserable.

But now is Christ risen from the dead, and become the firstfruits of them that slept.

For since by man came death, by man came also the resurrection of the dead. For as in Adam all die, even so in Christ shall all be made alive."

On Sand and in Stone

"Two friends were walking through the desert. During some point in the journey, they had an argument, and one friend slapped the other in the face.

The one who got slapped was hurt, but without saying anything, wrote in the sand:

'Today my best friend slapped me in the face.'

They kept on walking until they found an oasis, where they decided to take a swim. The one who had been slapped got stuck in the mire and started drowning, but the friend saved him.

After he recovered from the near drowning, he wrote on a stone:

'Today my best friend saved my life.'

The friend who had slapped and saved his best friend asked him, 'After I hurt you, you wrote in the sand; and now, you write on a stone, why?'

The other friend replied: 'When someone hurts us we should write it down in the sand where the winds of forgiveness can erase it away. But, when someone does something good for us, we must engrave it in stone where no wind can ever erase it.'"[13]

Learn to write your hurts in the sand and to carve your blessings in stone.

If You Know the Secret, Pass It On

Do you know the secret to lasting happiness and total satisfaction in life? Or are you among the millions who find every day to be a grind, such that you are barely making it at the end of the day? There's just not enough energy and zest in that tired body of yours to cope with the seemingly insurmountable demands that pile up increasingly day after day. Maybe you hope to finally discover a potion, an herbal concoction, or some kind of pill that will give you the answer to all of your needs.

> *Everyone is trying to find the secret to lasting happiness and total satisfaction with life.*

Everyone is trying to find the secret to lasting happiness and total satisfaction with life. You don't have to go very far in your quest. Someone wrote of a secret, and I am sharing the same with you.

The Secret

One day, one friend asked another,
'How is it that you are always happy?
You have so much energy,
And you never seem to get down.'
With her eyes smiling, she said,
'I know the Secret!'
'What Secret is that?'
To which she replied,
'I'll tell you all about it,
but you have to promise to
share the Secret with others.
The Secret is this:
I have learned there is little I can do
in my life that will make me truly happy.
I must depend on God to make

me happy and to meet my needs.
When a need arises in my life,
I have to trust God to supply
according to HIS riches.
I have learned most of the time
I don't need half of what I think I do.
He has never let me down.
Since I learned that 'Secret,' I am happy.'
The questioner's first thought was,
'That's too simple!'
But upon reflecting over her own life
she recalled how she thought
a bigger house would make her happy,
but it didn't!
She thought a better paying job would make her happy,
but it hadn't.
Where did she realize her greatest happiness?
Sitting on the floor with her grandchildren,
playing games, eating pizza or reading a story,
a simple gift from God."[14]

The Cross

We all wish that life could be a bed of roses—a carefree life without any worries or cares. "Bed of roses" is an English expression that represents a carefree life.[15] But, in real life, that usually isn't the case.

Sometimes, when life's problems become overwhelming, it helps to look around and see what other people are trying to cope with. You might find yourself far more fortunate than you imagined. Because, in reality, your trials may be so insignificant compared to what others are struggling with.

Jesus knows that everyone's life will, at some time, have burdens and problems. What can we do about that? Of course, Jesus has the answer! "And when he had called the people unto him…he said unto them, Whosoever will come after me, let him deny himself, and take up his cross, and follow me (Mark 8:34).

The Scriptures also say that God doesn't give us a cross that is heavier than what we can bear. The good Lord is not going to allow us to be tempted above what we are able to handle. But He will "with the temptation also make a way to escape," so that we are able to bear it" (1 Cor. 10:13).

Furthermore, crosses, burdens, and trials have a way of polishing us, strengthening our faith, and perfecting our characters. The apostle James says that we should count it all joy when we fall into diverse temptations knowing that the trying of our faith develops patience, and, when patience does its work, we will be "perfect and entire, wanting nothing" (James 1:2–4).

So when we are carrying a heavy burden—a cross—we know that it can help strengthen our faith. After all, Jesus carries all of our burdens if we ask Him to. When we are tempted to complain, consider this: When life is not a bed of roses, remember who wore the thorns.[16]

God Is a Refuge in Time of Trouble

At about 5:00 a.m. on a Monday morning, we were awakened by the sound of sirens in our neighborhood with urgent calls to immediately evacuate. It was a rude awakening, but we knew that danger was everywhere, and so we dutifully gathered some emergency clothes and supplies, hopped into our car, and fled the area.

Of course, we prayed that God would preserve our lives and protect our house—and those of countless others—from the hungry flames that were ravaging the hills. As it turned out, we saw from a distance many hours later how the wild winds had blown the flames to the west, and so we were able to return home that night.

Here are some lessons we learned from that experience!

Unlike Lot's wife, we did not take any time trying to decide whether or not to leave. We left our house and never looked back, putting everything in God's hands.

We have also found that, when one has total trust and confidence in God, it is easy to decide what to do. Just leave it with God, and you know He will do what is best for you.

We also want to take this opportunity to thank God, for He has been our refuge and strength, our help in time of trouble (Ps. 46:1).

It Matters Where You Look

One of the most spectacular demonstrations of Christ's control over nature was when He walked on the water to join His disciples in the boat one dark and stormy night on the Sea of Galilee. Peter, the ever-outspoken and adventurous disciple, asked Jesus if he could come out on the water, too, to meet Him. Everything seemed okay, until the Bible says, "But when he saw the wind boisterous, he was afraid; and beginning to sink, he cried, saying, 'Lord, save me' and Jesus stretched out His hand and pulled him up to safety (Matthew 14:30–31).

As we travel life's road, there will be trials and obstacles on the way that will make us stumble and fall. The enemy of our souls will bring discouragement upon us. And if we look at the boisterous winds and the angry waves as Peter did, we will become afraid and we could sink into the depths of despair. The secret is to look to Jesus and never take our gaze away from Him.

It matters where you look, be it on the sea or in your journey through life. When you look at your problems or your troubles, you can become discouraged. But when you look to Jesus and His blessings and the many little joyful things He puts around you, you'll make good progress and you'll get to your destination safely.

Here's a beautiful poem that urges us to look at the joyful things along the way.

The Joyful Things

At times I'm so discouraged
With problems of the day.
I fail to see the joyful things
That are along the way.

When troubles overwhelm me,
It's then my nerves may fray,
That's when I need to take the time
To simply sit and pray.

Reflecting on God's many gifts
Does make me so aware
Of all the joy in little things
Around me everywhere!

I must try to remember
Though problems come my way,
Not to miss the joyful things
And the beauty of the day.[17]

Judging Gently

Often in life we find ourselves passing judgment on the actions of people, and then later, when the truth comes to light, we realize we have been so terribly wrong. We feel so bad and terribly guilty. Because we can't read the heart, we don't know the motives that govern people's actions. That's why only God can judge. Because only He is able to know what's in a person's mind.

Consider the words of this poem.

Judge not the workings of his mind
And of his heart thou canst not see;
What looks to thy dim eyes a stain,
In God's pure light may only be
A scar, brought from some well-worn field,
Where thou wouldst only faint and yield.[18]

In the book of Matthew, we read that Jesus said, "Judge not, that ye be not judged. For with what judgment ye judge, ye shall be judged..." (Matt.7:1).

Christ Our Only Hope

Every so often, we need to be reminded about making our relationship with God sure and our mission here on earth in accordance with His will. So often, as we are caught up in the business of daily living, we neglect our spiritual lives. We get distracted by so many things, and, at times, we even get discouraged. So there is a need for us to pause every now and then in order to refocus on our goals, and, if need be, to restructure our priorities and lifestyles so that we can get back on track.

Consider these words carefully.

"You may go to heaven without health, without wealth, without honour, without pleasure, without friends, without learning; but you can never go to heaven without Christ."[19]

The bottom line is this: Do we have Christ in our hearts? Is He the center and focus of our everyday lives? If not, there is a work for us to do, which to me is most important.

The Holy Spirit can help us get back together with Christ, so that we can be sure of salvation and heaven.

A Lesson in Philosophy

"The following is the philosophy of Charles Schultz, the creator of the 'Peanuts' comic strip."[20]

Try to answer the following two sets of questions:

1. Name the five wealthiest people in the world.

2. Name the last five Heisman trophy winners.

3. Name the last five winners of the Miss America [Beauty Pageant].

4. Name ten people who have won the Nobel or Pulitzer Prize.

5. Name the last half dozen Academy Award winners for best actor and actress.

6. Name the last decade's worth of World Series winners.[21]

How did you fare in this quiz? Probably not very well! The point is this—we probably don't remember any of those people's names! And to think that they were once the best in their fields, captured the headlines in yesterday's newspapers, and were world-class celebrities. But, as they say, awards tarnish and achievements are forgotten.

"People do not care how much you know until they know how much you care."[22]

Now, answer this next set of questions.
1. List a few teachers who aided your journey through school.

2. Name three friends who helped you through a difficult time.

3. Name five people who have taught you something worthwhile.

4. Think of a few people who have made you feel appreciated and special.

5. Think of five people you enjoy spending time with.[23]

Of course, you can agree that the second set of questions was easier. And that's because the people who made a difference in your life were not the ones with the most credentials or the most money or the most awards. They were the ones who touched your life and showed you they cared.

This is in line with the good old truism that says, "People don't care how much you know until they know how much you care."[24]

And to think that this was what Jesus our Master did. "The Son of man came not to be ministered unto, but to minister, and to give his life a ransom for many" (Mark 10:45).

And is it any wonder that we love Him?

"Night Watch"[25]

A nurse took the tired, anxious serviceman to the bedside. "Your son is here," she said to the old man. She had to repeat the words several times before the patient's eyes opened. Heavily sedated because of the pain of his heart attack, he dimly saw the young uniformed Marine standing outside the oxygen tent. He reached out his hand.

The Marine wrapped his toughened fingers around the old man's limp ones, squeezing a message of love and encouragement. The nurse brought a chair so that the Marine could sit beside the bed. All through the night, the young Marine sat there in the poorly lighted ward, holding the old man's hand and offering him words of love and strength.

Occasionally, the nurse suggested that the Marine move away and rest awhile. He refused. Whenever the nurse came into the ward, the Marine was oblivious of her and of the night noises of the hospital—the clanking of the oxygen tank, the laughter of the night staff members exchanging greetings, the cries and moans of the other patients. Now and then she heard him say a few gentle words. The dying man said nothing, only held tightly to his son all through the night.

Along towards dawn, the old man died. The Marine released the now lifeless hand he had been holding and went to tell the nurse. While she did what she had to do, he waited. Finally, she returned. She started to offer words of sympathy, but the Marine interrupted her.

"Who was the man?" he asked.

The nurse was startled, "He was your father," she answered.

"No, he wasn't," the Marine replied. "I never saw him before in my life."

"Then why didn't you say something when I took you to him?"

"I knew right away there had been a mistake, but I also knew he needed his son, and his son just wasn't here. When I realized that he was too sick to tell whether or not I was his son, knowing how much he needed me, I stayed."

All around us are people in need of help—an encouraging word, a loving touch, a thoughtful deed—to let them know that they are loved. Will you be that person whom God can use to bring hope, peace, and joy to those bereft of such blessings?

If you agree, you will not have to go alone. God has promised to go with you and help you with this task. He says this in Isaiah 41:13 (NKJV): "For I, the Lord your God, will hold your right hand, saying to you, 'Fear not, I will help you.'"

"Be Still and Know…"[26]

One day a little girl slipped into her father's study. Without saying a word, she quietly sat on the floor close beside him, watching him at work.

After a while, he said, "Honey, is there something you want?"

"No," she replied, "I am just sitting here loving you."

Soon she left as quietly as she had come in…. She had not come to ask him for anything. She had just wanted to be near him and love him.

The thought came to him, "How often do we spend time in God's presence, just loving Him and becoming acquainted with Him? Or do I come to Him only when I have a request to ask of Him?"

The psalmist says, "Be still, and know that I am God…" Psalm 46:10. It is during those times—when we come to God without a list of things we want to have and without any petition to make—that God reveals Himself more fully to us. It is when we lose our souls in solitude and quietness in the Presence of God that we come to KNOW HIM not only as the powerful God who created the universe but also as a Friend—One who loves us so dearly that He wants us to be with Him forever.

As we live our lives, we need to create time for God. If you haven't already done so or if you did in the past but have neglected it due to the hustle and bustle of day-to-day living, why not decide now to carve out time for stillness and quietness in the presence of God from each 24-hour day. Use that time just to get to know Him and love Him as the Lord of your life.

The Power of Being

There is a story about a missionary who, lost at sea, was, by chance, washed up on the edge of a remote village. Half-dead from starvation, exposure to the seawater, he was found by the natives and was nursed back to health.

He then lived among these people for twenty years. And during that whole time, he confessed no faith. He didn't sing any songs. He didn't preach any sermons. He neither read nor recited any Scripture. He made no personal testimony about his faith. But when people were sick, he attended to them, sitting long into the night. When people were hungry, he gave them food. When people were lonely, he gave them company. He taught the ignorant. He was a source of enlightenment to those who were less knowledgeable. He always took the side of those who were wronged. There was not a single human condition with which he did not identify.

When missionaries later arrived at this island and began talking to the natives about a man called Jesus, the people insisted that the man they were talking about was among them and had lived with them for the past twenty years. The villagers led the missionaries to a hut, and there the missionaries found their long-lost fellow missionary whom they thought had died.

It is true that a well-ordered, well-disciplined life is still the most powerful argument in favor of Christianity. And it is still true that what we are can thunders so loud that people can't hear what we say. Our actions, not our words, are our most powerful witness!

Let us therefore put on Jesus Christ. And let us allow Him to live out His life within us. This is the secret to a powerful Christian life and witness.

To Judge or Not to Judge

"A grocery store checkout clerk once wrote to advice-columnist Ann Landers to complain that she had seen people buy "luxury" food items—like birthday cakes and bags of shrimp—with their food stamps. The writer went on to say that she thought all those people on welfare who treated themselves to such non-necessities were "lazy and wasteful."

A few weeks later, Landers' column was devoted entirely to people who had responded to the grocery clerk. One woman wrote:

I didn't buy a cake, but I did buy a big bag of shrimp with food stamps. So what? My husband had been working at a plant for fifteen years when it shut down. The shrimp casserole I made was for our wedding-anniversary dinner and lasted three days. Perhaps the grocery clerk that criticized that woman would have a different view of life after walking a mile in my shoes.

Another woman wrote:

I'm the woman who bought the $17 cake and paid for it with food stamps. I thought the checkout woman in the store would burn a hole through me with her eyes. What she didn't know is the cake was for my little girl's birthday. It will be her last. She has bone cancer and will probably be gone within six to eight months."[27]

An American Indian proverb, paraphrased, says: "Never judge a man until you have walked a mile in his moccasins.[28] So hold your judgment. You do not know the heart or even the circumstances surrounding a person's action, though the action may seem so obviously wrong.

And that is why only God can judge because He alone knows the motives of the heart. And Jesus Himself says: "Judge not, that ye be not judged" (Matt.7:1).

That Personal Touch

"A man stopped at a flower shop to order some flowers to be wired to his mother who lived two hundred miles away.

As he got out of his car, he noticed a young girl sitting on the curb sobbing. He asked her what was wrong and she replied: 'I wanted to buy a red rose for my mother. But I only have seventy-five cents, and a rose costs two dollars.' The man smiled and said, 'Come on in with me. I'll buy you a rose.'

He bought the little girl her rose and ordered his own mother's flowers. As they were leaving he offered the girl a ride home.

She said, 'Yes, please! You can take me to my mother.'

She directed him to a cemetery, where she placed the rose on a freshly dug grave.

The man returned to the flower shop, canceled the wire order, picked up a bouquet and drove the two hundred miles to his mother's home."[29]

Some of us may continue to feel obliged to cherish the memory of a loved one with expressions of love and affection even after the loved one is long gone. But how much better and more meaningful it would be if we expressed that love and care while the object of our affection is still able to see, hear, and feel our love.

Let us do that not only during special times but every day while we and those we love continue to have the breath of life within us.

Total Surrender

"A few centuries before Christ, Alexander the Great conquered almost all of the known world through sheer military strength, cleverness, and diplomacy. One day Alexander and a small company of soldiers approached a strongly defended, walled city. Alexander, standing outside the walls, raised his voice, demanding to see the king. The king, approaching the battlements above the invading army, agreed to hear Alexander's demands. 'Surrender to me immediately,' commanded Alexander. The king laughed. 'Why should I surrender to you?' he called down. 'We have you far outnumbered. You are no threat to us!' Alexander was ready to answer the challenge. 'Allow me to demonstrate why you should surrender,' he replied. Alexander ordered his men to line up single file and start marching. He marched them straight toward a sheer cliff that dropped hundreds of feet to the rocks below.

The king and his soldiers watched in shocked disbelief as, one by one, Alexander's soldiers marched without hesitation right off the cliff to their deaths. After ten soldiers had died, Alexander ordered the rest of the men to stop and to return to his side.

The king and his soldiers surrendered on the spot to Alexander the Great. The king and his soldiers realized that nothing would stop the eventual victory of men actually willing to give their lives for their leader."[30]

The question for us is this: Are we as obedient to our Lord Jesus Christ as those soldiers were to Alexander the Great? Are we so committed and dedicated to Him that we are willing to spend and be spent for the advancement of His kingdom on earth?

With such men and women of unflinching loyalty and devotion, how much power would He be able to exert through us and how soon the work of carrying the gospel to the world might be finished.

Valleys Don't Last Forever

Most of us are familiar with the twenty-third Psalm: "Yea, though I walk through the valley of the shadow of death, I will fear no evil; For You are with me" (Ps. 23:4, NKJV).

When David wrote these words, he was thinking about those who go through difficult experiences in life. As a matter of fact, one version of this psalm renders it this way, "Even if I walk through a very dark valley..." (Ps. 23:4, NHEB).

The word *dark* may describe a trying moment. It may mean a fiery trial or an ordeal that one might experience. It could be a terrible loss of assets or even of personal friends or loved ones. And it's a dark valley because you feel hemmed in by insurmountable odds, and the lights of hope are flickering or have probably even gone out altogether.

But this passage is a source of comfort because the psalmist says that God who is our Shepherd walks with us through the valley. He doesn't leave us alone. He is with us in the tempest and in the storm. And when the way gets too rough or too hard, He even picks us up and carries us in His bosom.

Finally, dark valleys do not last forever. God only allows us to walk in these valleys for a time—to build our trust in Him and to polish our characters for the time when we will walk in the society of heavenly beings. The verse says we walk through these dark valleys, but God promises that we will go past them and will soon find ourselves in green pastures and verdant meadows. And then goodness and mercy shall follow us all our days.

"A Woman and a Fork"[31]

"Eye has not seen, nor ear heard, nor have entered into the heart of man the things which God has prepared for those who love Him"
(1 Cor. 2:9, NKJV).

There was a young woman who had been diagnosed with a terminal illness and had been given three months to live. Therefore, as she was getting her things "in order," she contacted her [pastor] and had him come to her house to discuss certain aspects of her final wishes. She told him which songs she wanted sung at the service, what scriptures she would like read, and what outfit she wanted to be buried in.

Everything was in order and the [pastor] was preparing to leave when the young woman suddenly remembered something very important to her.

"There's one more thing," she said excitedly.

"What's that?" was the pastor's reply.

"This is very important," the young woman continued. "I want to be buried with a fork in my right hand."

The [pastor] stood looking at the young woman, not quite knowing what to say.

"That surprises you, doesn't it?" the young woman asked.

"Well, to be honest, I'm puzzled by the request," said the [pastor].

The young woman explained: "My grandmother once told me this story, and from there on out, I have always…tried to pass along its message to those I love and those who are in need of encouragement."

"In all my years of attending socials and dinners, I always remember that when the dishes of the main course were being cleared, someone would inevitably lean over and say, 'Keep your fork.' It was my favorite part because I knew that something better was coming…like velvety chocolate cake or deep-dish apple pie. Something wonderful, and with substance!" So, I just want people to see me there in the casket with a fork in my hand and I want them to wonder, 'What's with the fork?' Then I want you to tell them: 'Keep your fork…the best is yet to come.'"

The [pastor's] eyes welled up with tears of joy as he hugged the young woman good-bye. He knew this would be one of the last times he would see her before her death. But he also knew that the young woman had a better grasp of heaven than he did. She had a better grasp of what heaven would be like than many people twice her age, with twice as much experience and knowledge. She KNEW that something better was coming.

At the funeral, people were walking by the young woman's casket, and they saw the cloak she was wearing and the fork placed in her right hand. Over and over, the [pastor] heard the question, "What's with the fork?" And over and over, he smiled.

I want you to tell them: 'Keep your fork...the best is yet to come.'

During his message, the [pastor] told the people of the conversation he had with the young woman shortly before she died. He also told them about the fork and about what it symbolized to her. The [pastor] told the people how he could not stop thinking about the fork and told them that they probably would not be able to stop thinking about it either. He was right."

If things are going great, don't be tempted to settle down and think this is all you need, because the best is yet to come. And know that, whatever life offers you, it will never get you anywhere near where what God has in store for you. The apostle Paul declares:

"Eye has not seen, nor ear heard, nor have entered into the heart of man the things which God has prepared for those who love Him" (1 Cor. 2:9, NKJV).

"The Brick"[32]

A young and successful executive was traveling down a neighborhood street, going a bit too fast in his new Jaguar. He was watching for kids darting out from between parked cars and slowed down when he thought he saw something. As his car passed, no children appeared. Instead a brick smashed into the Jag's side door! He slammed on the brakes and backed the Jag back to the spot where the brick had been thrown.

The angry driver then jumped out of the car, grabbed the nearest kid and pushed him up against a parked car, shouting, "What was that all about and who are you?...That's a new car and that brick you threw is going to cost a lot of money? Why did you do it?"

The young boy was apologetic. "Please mister...please, I'm sorry but I didn't know what else to do," he pleaded. "I threw the brick because no one else would stop."

With tears dripping down his face and off his chin, the youth pointed to a spot just around a parked car. "It's my brother," he said. "He rolled off the curb and fell out of his wheelchair and I can't lift him up."

Now sobbing, the boy asked the stunned executive, "Would you please help me get him back into his wheelchair? He's hurt and he's too heavy for me."

Moved beyond words, the driver tried to swallow the rapidly swelling lump in his throat. He hurriedly lifted the handicapped boy back into the wheelchair, then took out a linen handkerchief and dabbed at the fresh scrapes and cuts. A quick look told him everything was going to be okay.

"Thank you and may God bless you," the grateful child told the stranger. Too [shaken] for words, the man simply watched the boy push his wheelchair-bound brother down the sidewalk toward their home.

It was a long, slow walk back to the Jaguar. The damage was very noticeable, but the driver never bothered to repair the dented side door. He kept the dent [in his car to remind him of the important lesson he learned that day].

The questions we may ask ourselves are these: Are we going so fast in life that someone who may be in need has to throw a brick at us in order to get our attention? Are we too focused on our personal lives and concerns that we have become desensitized to the suffering of a needy world?

God is constantly trying to get our attention, and sometimes He may throw a brick at us and at our possessions so that we will stop to listen and get His message for us.

Growth Time in the Valley

In life, we experience sunshine and shadow, the bitter and the sweet, joys and sorrows, and mountains and valleys. It's the variety and the contrast that give life balance on this side of heaven and make life a wonderful thing. Even seeming difficulties can prove to be a blessing: storm clouds forming at dusk make a spectacular sunset.

> *Thank you for the valleys, Lord, so I can learn and grow close to You.*

More than anything, it's time spent in the valleys, when the sun can't shine through the clouds—that is when we come under the shadow of pain and loss that we experience growth. It is during these times that we develop muscles in our spiritual lives and we receive a polishing and a strengthening that prepare us for greater things ahead and for a future life in glory. The following is a poem that speaks to this point. Thank you for the valleys, Lord, so I can learn and grow close to You.

It's in the Valleys I Grow

Sometimes life seems hard to bear,
Full of sorrow, trouble and woe.
It's then I have to remember
That it's in the valleys I grow.

If I always stayed on the mountain top
And never experienced pain,
I would never appreciate God's love
And would be living in vain.

I have so much to learn
And my growth is very slow;
Sometimes I need the mountain tops
But it's in the valleys I grow.

I do not always understand
Why things happen as they do,
But I am very sure of one thing.
My Lord will see me through.

My little valleys are nothing
When I picture Christ on the cross.
He went through the valley of death;
His victory was Satan's loss.

Forgive me Lord, for complaining
When I'm feeling so very low.
Just give me a gentle reminder
That it's in the valleys I grow.

Continue to strengthen me, Lord
And use my life each day
To share your love with others
And help them find their find their way.

Thank you for valleys, Lord, For this one thing I know
The mountain tops are glorious
But, it's in the valleys I grow!"[33]

Love Finds a Way

"A man was trying to read a serious book, but his little boy kept interrupting him. He would lean against his knees and say, 'Daddy, I love you.'

The father would give him a pat and say rather absently, 'Yes, son, I love you too.' And he would kind of give him a little push away so he could keep on reading.

But this didn't satisfy the boy. And finally he ran to his father and said, 'I love you, daddy.' And he jumped up on his lap and threw his arms around him and gave him a big squeeze, explaining, 'And I've just got to DO something about it! (emphasis added)'"[34]

As we grow in love, we aren't content with small-talk love or pat-on-the-head love. We want to get involved and "do something about it." Jesus says in John 14:15 (NKJV), "If you love Me, keep My commandments."

If we truly love the Lord, we will find ways to express our love by doing and keeping His Words. Just like the parable of the two sons, told by Jesus Himself. When the Father told the first son to go work in the vineyard, that son said, "I will not," but later he regretted it and went. He asked the same of the second son who said, "Yes," but later did not go. The first son proved his love and respect for his father because, although he was unwilling to go as commanded early on, he changed his mind and went.

May we prove our love by doing what God has commanded us to do and by going where He has commanded us to go.

How to be Happy

Author Sonja Lyubomirsky[35] says that there are specific factors that contribute to a person's happiness: 50% are from factors determined by genetics, 10% are from circumstances (such as divorce or a financial windfall), and the remaining 40% are from factors that are entirely within the person's control.

Since so much of a person's happiness comes from factors that are within his or her control, she goes on to suggest intervention remedies that are sure to help bring happiness. The following are examples of these remedies:

1. Write letters of gratitude.
2. Perform conscious acts of kindness.
3. Keep a "best possible self" journal.
4. Outline future goals for six or more weeks.
5. Don't overthink it. When stewing about something, stop. Set aside thirty minutes late in the day to do nothing but ruminate.
6. Learn good coping skills. Write down traumatic experiences. Learn how to recognize and argue with overly pessimistic thoughts.
7. Savor life's joys. Relish ordinary experiences, like a good meal or a hot shower.
8. Conjure up favorite memories when you're down.
9. Cultivate optimism. Share favorite parts of your day.

What she further suggests is to know when one may have to seek medication or therapy for the state of unhappiness or "depression" that a person may find herself/himself in.

The following are telltale signs that should prod one to seek professional help:

1. Sad mood. Feeling anxious or empty for most of the day.

2. Loss of interest. Finding less pleasure in activities you used to enjoy.

3. Fatigue. Having less energy with trouble sleeping or oversleeping.

4. Fuzzy focus. Having difficulty concentrating.

When one experiences these symptoms, it is time to get clinical help.

Of course, you can always go to Someone who can help you because He (Jesus) cares for you. The apostle Peter says, "Casting all your care upon him; for He cares for you" (1 Peter 5:7, NKJV).

Put Down Your Burdens

"A professor was giving a lecture on stress management. He raised a glass of water and asked the audience, 'How heavy do you think this glass of water is?' The answers ranged from a half-pound to three pounds.

'It does not matter about the absolute weight. It depends on how long you hold it. If I hold it for a minute, it is OK. If I hold it for an hour, I will have an ache in my right arm. If I hold it for a day, the pain will be intolerable. It is the exact same weight, but the longer I hold it, the heavier it becomes. If we carry our burdens all the time, sooner or later, we will not be able to carry on—our burdens become increasingly heavier.

What you have to do is to put the glass down, rest for a while (say a prayer) before holding it up again. We have to put down the burden of life periodically, so that we can be refreshed and are able to carry on. So before you return home from work tonight, put down the burden of work."[36]

> *If we carry our burdens all the time, sooner or later, we will not be able to carry on—our burdens become increasingly heavier.*

Whatever burden you have now on your shoulders, let it down for a moment if you can. Pick it up again later, when you have rested.... Rest and relax.

And that is why, in God's wonderful plan, He gave us the night so that we can have time to lay down the burdens of the day. And that is the reason He gave us the Sabbath—so we can have time to lay down the burdens of the week. But most of all, that is why we have Jesus—so that we can have someone to cast our burdens upon, whatever they are and whenever we need to lay them down.

The Scriptures say: "Casting all your care upon Him, for He cares for you" (1 Peter 5:7, NKJV).

Twice Owned

"A boy made a little boat. "One day, with exuberant anticipation, he carried his boat to the shore of the lake and sailed it on the clear, blue water. The little boat skimmed along as the gentle breeze blew its sails across the rippling waves.

Then suddenly, a gust of wind caught the little boat and snapped the string the boy was holding. Out farther and farther the little boat sailed until at last it vanished from sight. Sadly, the boy made his way home—without his prized possession. It was lost.

The weeks and months went by. Then one day as the boy passed a toy shop, something caught his attention. Could it be? Was it really? He looked closer. It was. Yes, there in the display window was his own little boat.

Overjoyed, the boy bolted into the store and told the owner about the boat on display. It really belonged to him. He had made it, hadn't he?

'I'm sorry,' the shopkeeper said, 'but it's my boat now. If you want it, you'll have to pay the price for it.'

Sad at heart, the boy left the store. But he was determined to get his boat back, even though it meant working and saving until he had enough money to pay for it.

At last the day came. Clutching his money in his fist, he walked into the shop and spread his hard-earned money on the countertop.

'I've come back to buy my boat,' the boy said.

The clerk counted the money. It was enough. Reaching into the showcase, the storekeeper took the boat and handed it to the eager boy. The lad's face lit up with a smile of satisfaction as he held the little boat in his arms.

'You're mine,' he said, 'twice mine. Mine because I made you, and now, mine because I bought you.'"[37]

The story of this little boy reminds us about what God did to make us His prized possession once again. He owns us first by creation. And then, when we sold ourselves to the devil, He bought us back with the precious blood of Jesus. Like the little boy in our story, God says to us today, "You are twice mine. Mine because I made you; and now, mine because I bought you with My blood."

Ways to Reduce Stress in Our Lives

We live stress-filled lives. And this is understandable because the amount of stress we experience is often directly proportional to the degree of difficulty or the size of challenges we face in life. Often these are beyond our control. But what we can control is how we respond to them. We should not allow stress to dominate our lives, nor should we allow it to stay for so long.

Jesus said, "Take therefore no thought for the morrow: for the morrow shall take thought for the things of itself. Sufficient unto the day is the evil thereof" (Matt. 6:34). We should live one day at a time. Borrowing from tomorrow's burdens can put us into overload. That's why we have medical problems such as heart attacks, strokes, and hypertension. And, as for the problems of today, we should be able to face up to them and find a way to live through them with God's help.

A friend sent me the following material which is a very good way of helping us live our lives from day to day and thus reduce the amount of stress we have to deal with.

It is entitled, "36 Christian Ways to Reduce Stress."[38]

1. Pray.

2. Go to bed on time.

3. Get up on time, so you can start the day unrushed.

4. Say "No" to projects/activities that won't fit into your time schedule, or that will compromise your mental health.

5. Delegate tasks to capable others.

6. Simplify and unclutter your life.

7. Less is more. (Although one is often not enough, two are often too many.)

8. Allow extra time to do things and to get to places.

9. Pace yourself. Spread out big changes and difficult projects

over time. Don't lump the hard things all together.

10. Take one day at a time.
11. Separate worries from concerns. If a situation is a concern, find out what God would have you do and let go of the anxiety. If you can't do anything about a situation, forget it.
12. Live within your budget. (Don't use credit cards for purchases.)
13. Have backups: an extra car key in your wallet, an extra house key buried in the garden, extra stamps, etc.
14. K.M.S. (Keep Mouth Shut). This single piece of advice can prevent an enormous amount of trouble.
15. Do something for the Kid in You every day.
16. Carry a Bible with you to read while waiting in line.
17. Get enough exercise.
18. Eat right.
19. Get organized, so everything has its place.
20. Listen[ing to music] while driving that can help improve your quality of life.
21. Write down thoughts and inspirations. (This means that we should always carry a pen and note pad with us. Some of these brilliant thoughts hit us during odd moments and, if we don't capture them in ink at their moment of revelation, we could lose them forever.)
22. Every day, find time to be alone.
23. Having problems? Talk to God on the spot. Try to nip small problems in the bud. Don't wait until it's time to go to bed to try and pray.
24. Make friends with godly people.
25. Keep a folder of favorite Scriptures on hand.

26. Remember that the shortest bridge between despair and hope is often a good "Thank you, Jesus!"

27. Laugh.

28. Laugh some more!

29. Take your work seriously, but not yourself at all.

30. Develop a forgiving attitude. (Most people are doing the best they can.)

31. Be kind to unkind people. (They probably need it the most.)

32. Sit on your ego.

33. Talk less; listen more.

34. Slow down.

35. Remind yourself that you are not the general manager of the universe.

36. Every night before bed, think of one thing you're grateful for that you've never been grateful for before.

Remember, God has a way of turning things around for you. "If God is for us, who can be against us?" (Rom. 8:31, NKJV).

The Bible also says, "Thou wilt keep him in perfect peace, whose mind is stayed on thee: because he trusteth in thee" (Isa. 26:3).

Having the mind stayed on Jesus and trusting in Him drives away stress in our lives and allows us to have peace, sweet peace.

Do You Know Yourself?

One of the most important tasks in life—next to knowing God—is to know one's self. Various ancient Greek philosophers, including Socrates, are credited with saying, "Know thyself."[39]

Especially in the realm of the spiritual, we tend to esteem ourselves more highly than we ought to. And that is because, in most cases, we compare ourselves to many of our erring brethren or to an ethical standard that is so much lower than what God requires of us.

The prophet Jeremiah says, "The heart is deceitful above all things, and desperately wicked: who can know it?" (Jer. 17:9). Like the older brother in the parable of the prodigal son, we scoff at our younger brethren who have gone to a far country and wasted their inheritance with prodigal living, but we do not realize that—although we haven't physically left the church— our hearts have gone far away from Him.

So, do we know ourselves? A.W. Tozer suggests a way by which we can take a hint about who or what we really are. He says that we can be known by the following ("The 7 Rules for Self-Discovery"):

"1. What we want most.

2. What we think about most.

3. How we use our money.

4. What we do with our leisure time.

5. The company we enjoy.

6. Who and what we admire.

7. What we laugh at."[40]

We may also need to say the prayer of the psalmist David, when he said, "Search me, O God, and know my heart: try me, and know my thoughts: And see if there be any wicked way in me, and lead me in the way everlasting" (Ps. 139:23–24).

The Tater People

We were having a committee meeting to fill some vacancies in a number of positions for ministry responsibilities within the church. Some names were suggested, but the committee was hesitant to accept those nominations because of what it felt was an inadequacy due to a lack of experience and training in the particular field of need.

Eventually, the committee members accepted the nominations after they heard these words of encouragement:

"God doesn't call the qualified, He qualifies the called."[41]

"It's not your ability but your availability"[42] that matters in the eyes of God.

"All His [God's] biddings are enablings."[43]

> *There are those who are always prepared to stop whatever they are doing to lend a helping hand. They bring sunshine into the lives of others.*

There are those who are always prepared to stop whatever they are doing to lend a helping hand. They bring sunshine into the lives of others.

In connection with the above, I want to share a poem that puts people in church into certain categories. It's called "The Tater People."[44]

Some people never seem motivated to participate but are just content to watch while others do the work.

They are called "Spec Taters."

Some people never do anything to help, but are gifted at finding fault with the way others do the work.

They are called "Comment Taters."

Some people are very bossy and like to tell others what to do, but don't want to soil their own hands.

They are called "Dick Taters."

Some people are always looking to cause problems by asking others to agree with them. It is too hot or too cold, too sour or too sweet.

They are called "Agie Taters."

There are those who say they will help, but somehow just never get around to actually doing the promised help.

They are called "Hezzie Taters."

Some people can put up a front and pretend to be someone they are not.

They are called "Emma Taters."

Then there are those who love others and do what they say they will. They are always prepared to stop whatever they are doing and lend a helping hand. They bring real sunshine into the lives of others.

They are called "Sweet Taters."

They say, "Variety is the very spice of life,"[45] but I'd rather have everybody in church be a "Sweet Tater." Because I love "Sweet Taters."

Making a Difference

In his book, *Seeds of Greatness*,[46] Dennis Waitley tells this story about how one person can make a difference.

"A businessman and his wife who were busy to the point of exhaustion. They were committed to each other, their family, their church, their work, and their friends.

Needing a break, they escaped for a few days of relaxation at an oceanfront hotel. One night, a violent storm lashed the beach and sent massive breakers thundering against the shore. The man lay in his bed listening and thinking about his own stormy life of never-ending demands and pressures.

The wind finally died down and shortly before daybreak the man slipped out of bed and took a walk along the beach to see what damage had been done. As he strolled, he saw that the beach was covered with starfish that had been thrown ashore and helplessly stranded by the great waves. Once the morning sun burned through the clouds, the starfish would dry out and die.

Suddenly, the man saw an interesting sight. A young boy who had also noticed the plight of the starfish was picking them up, one at a time, and flinging them back into the ocean.

'Why are you doing that?' the man asked the lad as he got close enough to be heard. 'Can't you see that one person will never make a difference— you'll never be able to get all those starfish back into the water? There are just too many.'

'Yes, that's true,' the boy sighed as he bent over and picked up another and tossed it back into the water. Then as he watched it sink, he looked at the man, and smiled, and said, 'But it sure made a difference to that one.'

We have all been commissioned by our Lord to go into the trenches of the world, see the great need, and be change-agents for Him. As we look at the magnitude of our task and the seemingly meager resources we have at our disposal to accomplish our mission, we may feel a bit discouraged, but we should not allow this to happen. Let us move on and continue to do our work, changing the world one person at a time.

And as we go, Jesus promises His Presence with us, saying, "…and lo, I am with you always, even to the end of the age" (Matt. 28:20, NKJV).

The Need to Be Positive

A young boy was fishing in the river when a man came along. When the man asked how many fish the boy had caught, he replied: "If I catch this fish that is nibbling at my bait right now, that will be one; plus two more will make it three!"

We might say that the boy had an interesting way of saying *zero* or *nothing*. But there is virtue in looking at things in their most favorable light and saying positive things. Call this "optimism" or "positivism." It is something we need to cultivate and have more of.

Consider how small positive thoughts can eventually affect your life.

"Keep your thoughts positive, because your thoughts become your words.

Keep your words positive, because your words become your behavior.

Keep your behavior positive, because your behavior becomes your habits.

Keep your habits positive, because your habits become your values.

Keep your values positive, because your values become your destiny."[47]

In the Cross of Christ

In *101 Hymn Stories*, Kenneth Osbeck tells this beautiful story about the cross of Jesus.

"Centuries ago on the South Coast of China, high up on a hill overlooking the harbor of Macao, Portuguese settlers built an enormous cathedral. They believed it would weather time, and they placed upon the front wall of this cathedral a massive bronze cross that stood high into the sky.

Not too many years later, a typhoon came and God's fingerwork swept away man's handiwork, and all of that cathedral was pushed into the ocean and down the hill as debris, except the front wall and that bronze cross that stood high.

Centuries later, there was a shipwreck out a little beyond that harbor. And some died and a few lived. One of the men that was hanging onto wreckage from the ship, moving up and down in the crest of the ocean as the swells were moving, was disoriented, frightened, and he didn't know where land was. As he would come up on the swell, he'd spot that cross, tiny from that distance. His name was Sir John Bowring.

When he made it to land and lived to tell the story, he wrote,

In the cross of Christ I glory,
Towering o'er the wrecks of time;
All the light of sacred story
Gathers round its head sublime.

And the last stanza.

When the woes of life o'er take me,
Hopes deceive, and fears annoy,
Never shall the cross forsake me;
Lo! it glows with peace and joy.[48]

John Bowring is telling us that we have a cross, and we have an altar. And when all of life seems to crush in on top of us, we just need to go back to the Cross and remember the empty tomb. Call to mind the fact that

that Man is neither on the Cross nor in the tomb, but that He lives and He stands ready and able to give us victory over whatever we are going through at the time.

Come by grace to the Cross and say, "That is my sufficiency. That is my only hope."

May we all have a better understanding and appreciation of the wondrous cross of Jesus. And may we be able to say with John Bowring, "In the cross of Christ I glory."[49]

Advice for a Happy Life

My family and I were in Evansville, Indiana, for graduation exercises, which were the culmination of my completing a three-year doctoral program in Biblical Studies with the goal to make me more effective in my ministry for the Lord.

We had our special moments while in Evansville. I didn't know what to expect, but the celebration and fellowship of the commencement exercises far exceeded my expectations. Master's International School of Divinity graduated fifty-seven students that year—twenty-eight with doctoral degrees and the rest with bachelor's and master's degrees. What was so inspiring to me were some of the stories behind the scenes—how some of the candidates had worked to reach the pinnacle of their academic achievements. These were stories of dedication and commitment, of determination and endurance, and of courage and hope in the face of seemingly insurmountable obstacles.

There was an eighty-five-year-old man who finally earned his degree and was recognized with an "Academic Endurance" award. There was a couple who graduated with their master's degrees together with their daughter—which earned them the "Yokefellow Award." Also among the candidates was a lady who had been diagnosed with cancer after she registered for the program. She finished the requirements of her doctoral degree in between chemotherapy and radiation treatments, and the school recognized her with a "Conqueror's Award."

> *Keep trusting in God. He will see you through all the challenges that come your way.*

Some may think that these are examples of much ado about nothing. But one does not apply himself or herself or give his or her all just so he or she can add a few letters after his or her name. Nor does one do it so he or she can earn bragging rights. It is simply a situation of one heeding the counsel of Paul when he says to the young Timothy, "Study to shew thyself approved unto God, a workman that needeth not to be ashamed, rightly dividing the word of truth" (2 Tim. 2:15). Keep trusting in God. He will see you through all the challenges that come your way.

I want to share with you some advice that I came across in my reading—advice that will help you live a happy life if you give heed to it.

"1. Celebrate life.

2. Have courage amidst fear....

3. Be positive.

4. Smile a lot.

5. Don't worry, be happy.

6. Treat others with respect.

7. Keep your promises.

8. Be honest and faithful!"[50]

And I want to add another one which is this: Keep trusting in God. He will see you through all the challenges that come your way.

God's Ways Are Best

Have there been times that you prayed, but the Lord did not answer in the way you wanted Him to? Maybe God's answer to your prayer was the exact opposite of what you asked for. You may even have waited—to the point that you wondered whether God was powerful enough to make things happen for you. Maybe you even thought that God was ignoring or snubbing you.

More than a century ago, a Confederate soldier wrote these words.

Prayer of a Confederate Soldier

I asked God for strength that I might achieve.
I was made weak that I might learn to obey.
I asked for health that I might do great things.
I was given infirmity that I might do better things.
I asked for riches that I might be happy.
I was given poverty that I might be wise.
I asked for power that I might have the praise of men.
I was given weakness that I might feel the need of God.
I asked for all things that I might enjoy life.
I was given life that I might enjoy all things.
I got nothing that I asked for—but everything that I had hoped for.
Almost despite myself, my unspoken prayers were answered.
I am, among all men, most richly blessed.[51]

We may not always immediately realize it but, upon more considerable thought, when the emotions have died down and the smoke has cleared, we find that God's ways are still best!

God's Hand

From our own experiences, each of us must know how good the hand of God is. The following poem by Edward Bok should be a source of strength to all Christians.

God's Hand

Father so gentle, take Thou my hand;
Deep are the waters, I know not the way;
Sleepless the nights, confused is the day;
All is so empty, so lone do I stand.

God, I believe, but the burden is sore,
Faith and fresh courage are all I implore.
Give calm to my heart, that will banish all fear.
Open Thou my eyes, that Thy purpose may be clear.

Answer my wonder, dispel all my doubt,
Teach me the lesson of doing without.
Tho' hard be the cross, with help I can stand,
Father so gentle, I reach out my hand.

Hearken, my child: believe in My Word;
Surrender thyself to Me: I am thy Lord;
Earth's deepest sorrows, they last but a day;
Fresh courage I will give you: I am the way.

Look up and trust! For the sun shines on high;
No shadow lies there; clear blue is the sky.
On guard are the stars, bringing calm to thy sleep;
Learn peace; have faith that thy watch I will keep.

Dry now thy tears,
Make thy heart bright with cheer,
Have faith! I am near, at thy side do I stand,
I am thy guide, put thy trust in My hand."[52]

Yes, God's hand is God's Spirit extended to each of us today. That Hand will sustain us in every hour of trial. It will guide us around the pitfalls of Satan. Let's clasp that Hand and never let it go, and He will lead us to the kingdom of God.

An Intercontinental Journey

My travels have taken me across three continents recently: Africa, Europe, and America.

No, I didn't go on an African safari—the one where you secure yourself in a motorized "cage" as you feast your eyes on wildlife going about their activities in their natural habitat.

The part of Africa that I visited was Morocco, a country sitting on the northern tip of the continent, just along the coast of the Mediterranean and the Atlantic. In fact, in the city of Tangier, the waters of both the Mediterranean and Atlantic meet!

Forget about stereotyped images of Africa that have long been planted in your mind— images of mud huts and sand dunes and camel caravans. This portion of Africa happens to be blessed with lush vegetation and fertile farmlands. Along the roads, farmers were busy harvesting their corn and peanuts and melons. And the roadsides were literally dotted with piles and piles of produce (honeydew melons, yellow melons, etc.) for the local and foreign consumer. Tangier and Casablanca were impressive, with their elite housing for the many Middle Eastern royalty who come flocking to their white-sand beaches.

In Europe, Spain and Portugal still have so much of the Old World influence in them. Visiting these countries is like going back 500 or 600 years in time when both were world superpowers in the areas of navigation and maritime science. We saw the tower—and it still stands as a museum today—in Lisbon, Portugal, where every ship going out to discover new worlds was formally launched and blessed as it left the mouth of the river and plunged into the waters of the Atlantic.

We saw the tombs of famous nautical heroes—Vasco da Gama, Sebastián del Cano, and Christopher Columbus. Magellan's body is not buried there because he was killed by Lapu-Lapu, the Mactan ruler, on Cebu island in the Philippines.)

There were monuments memorializing the discovery of America and the New World by Columbus, and we saw the magnificent throne room at the Alhambra Palace in Granada where King Ferdinand and Queen Isabella received him following his successful voyage.

One might say that all the honor and credit given to these men were richly deserved. Considering that these men lived at a time when it was believed that the earth was flat and sailing to the edge of it could plunge you into an unfathomable abyss. These were hardy and courageous men. They had leadership and determination. They might sail out in one or two vessels with hundreds of men only to come back a year or two later with just one ship left and a few scores of men, their numbers having been decimated by disease and war with hostile natives.

And to think that, today, all one does is get a ticket, board a Boeing 747, crisscross the continents, and come back to work in two weeks.

Times have changed! And this in fulfillment of prophecy. In Daniel 12:4, the angel Gabriel tells Daniel, "...seal the book, even to the time of the end: many shall run to and fro, and knowledge shall be increased."

We live in the time of the end. Knowledge has increased, particularly in the area of communication and travel. Are we using this increase in knowledge to accomplish our mission? Are we making sure that our lives are a witness to others of the end times that we live in?

Just a Little More

Sometimes we become oblivious to the fact that God has placed us here on this earth for a special purpose. We have a task to do—one that can only be done by us and no one else. We are change- agents. We are here to impact others for good. He wants us to go make a difference in the lives of those who, by His Divine Providence, have come within the sphere of our influence. Even the little things that we do, when blessed by the Lord, will accomplish much for His glory.

> *Even the little things that we do, when blessed by the Lord, will accomplish much for His glory.*

Did He not say that we are the salt of the earth? And again, that we are the light of the world? That's why we are instructed to "…let your light so shine before men, that they may see your good works, and glorify your Father which is in heaven" (Matt. 5:13–16).

We should not neglect to use our God-given opportunities to serve as the salt of the earth or the light of the world, no matter how small the contribution may seem to us. For even the little things that we do, when blessed by the Lord, will accomplish much for His glory.

A little more happiness spread through the day,
A little more cheer to light up the way;
A little more thought for the chap at our side,
A little more credit for others who've tried….

A little more kindness in word and in deed,
A little more boosting that others may need.
A little more love for the folks that we know,
A little more effort so friendships may grow.

Just a little of these as we plod along here,
Will make it a wonderful, wonderful year.[53]

This Too Shall Pass

This story is from Jewish lore. It is about wise King Solomon and one of his ministers. It helps us relate to our present circumstances and allows us to deal successfully with the things life brings to us.

"One day Solomon decided to humble Benaiah [ben Yehoyada, his most trusted minister] to put an end to his boasting. So he summoned his minister and said to him, 'Benaiah, there is a certain ring that I want you to find and bring to me. I wish to wear it for Sukkot. That gives you six months to find it.'

'If it exists anywhere on earth, your majesty,' replied Benaiah, 'I will find it and bring it to you! But what makes this ring so special?'

The king answered, 'If a happy man looks at it, he becomes sad, and if a sad man looks at it, he becomes happy.'

Now Solomon knew that no such ring existed in the world, but he wished to give his minister a little taste of humility....

Spring passed and then summer, and still Benaiah had no idea where he could find the ring....

On the night before Sukkot, he decided to take a walk in one of the poorest quarters of Jerusalem.... He passed by a young merchant who had just begun to set out the day's wares on a shabby carpet.

'Have you by any chance heard of a ring that makes the happy wearer forget his joy and the broken-hearted wearer forget his sorrows?" asked Benaiah. The young merchant shook his head. But nearby, his grandfather overheard Benaiah's question.... He whispered something in his grandson's ear. 'Wait!' he called out to Benaiah.

He watched the man take a plain gold ring from his carpet and engrave something on it. But, when Benaiah read the words engraved on the ring, his face broke out in a wide smile....

That night the entire city welcomed in the holiday of Sukkot with great festivity. 'Well, my friend,' said Solomon, 'have you found what I sent you after?'

All the ministers laughed, and Solomon himself smiled....

To everyone's surprise, Benaiah held up a small gold ring and declared, 'Here it is, your majesty!'

As soon as Solomon read the inscription, the smile vanished from his face. The merchant had written three Hebrew letters on the gold band: *gimel, zayin, yud*, which began the words *Gam zeh yáavor*—meaning, 'This too shall pass.'

At the moment Solomon realized that all his wisdom and fabulous wealth and tremendous power were but fleeting things, for one day he would be nothing but dust...."[54]

So, if success is at our fingertips, and everything we touch seems to turn to gold; if we feel like we are sitting on top of the world; let us not think this is going to be forever—for "this too shall pass."

It could be the calm before the storm—the seven years of plenty which is going to be followed by the seven years of famine, as it was in Pharaoh's dream.

And if, at the moment, we are experiencing hardship and difficulty, let us remember that "this too shall pass." This is not going to be forever. So don't be discouraged. And do not give up.

So hang in there, because "this too shall pass."

A Journey Through Life

Life is a journey. But it is also a school where we learn and become educated. And if our ears, eyes, and hearts are open every time, we can learn the many lessons life wants to teach us as we travel along. Here is something I want to share with you to see if you have already learned these bits of truth about life.

I've learned that:

"…you can do something in an instant that will give you heartache for life.

…it's taking me a long time to become the person I want to be.

…you should always leave loved ones with loving words. It may be the last time you see them.

…you can keep going long after you think you can't.

…we are responsible for what we do, no matter how we feel.

…either you control your attitude or it controls you."[55]

"…regardless of how hot and steamy a relationship is at first, the passion fades and there had better be something else to take its place.

…heroes are the people who do what has to be done when it needs to be done, regardless of the consequences.

…money is a lousy way of keeping score.

…my best friend and I can do anything or nothing and have the best time."

…sometimes when I'm angry, I have the right to be angry, but that doesn't give me the right to be cruel.

...true friendship continues to grow, even over the longest distance. Same goes for true love....

...just because someone doesn't love you the way you want them to doesn't mean they don't love you with all they have.

...maturity has more to do with what types of experiences you've had, and what you've learned from them and less to do with how many birthdays you've celebrated."[56]

"...your family won't always be there for you. It may seem funny, but people you aren't related to can take care of you and love you and teach you to trust people again. Families aren't biological."[57]

"...no matter how good a friend is, they're going to hurt you every once in a while and you must forgive them for that.

...it isn't always enough to be forgiven by others, sometimes you have to learn to forgive yourself.

...our background and circumstances may have influenced who we are, but we are responsible for who we become.

...just because two people argue, it doesn't mean they don't love each other. And just because they don't argue, it doesn't mean they do.

...we don't have to change friends if we understand that friends change.

...you shouldn't be so eager to find out a secret, it could change your life forever.

...two people can look at the exact same thing and see something totally different.

...your life can be changed in a matter of hours by people who don't even know you.

…even when you think you have no more to give, when a friend cries out to you, you will find the strength to help.

…credentials on the wall do not make you a decent human being.

…the people you care about most in life are taken from you too soon."[58]

I trust that we are learning as we move along. And there could be a lot more awaiting us as we experience life and continue around the next bend."

Helpful Hints for Relaxation in the Lord

In our day and age, with society hustling and bustling about, it is easy to get caught up in worry and anxiety. Demands from work and school life can be a burden at times. We want to have time and energy to spend time with the more important things in life, such as family. Here are some tips to help you in your quest for more rest and relaxation.

Eighteen Proven Stress Reducers

1. Don't rely on your memory. Write down appointments, when to pick up the laundry, when library books are due, etc.

2. Get up 15 minutes earlier in the morning so you don't start the day feeling frazzled.

3. Keep a duplicate car key in your wallet.

4. An instant cure for most stress: thirty minutes of brisk walking or other aerobic exercise.

5. Resolve to be tender with the young, compassionate with the aged, sympathetic with the striving, and tolerant with the weak and erring, for some time in life you will have been all of these.

6. Say 'No, thank you' to extra projects you don't have the time or energy for.

7. Set up contingency plans—just in case, 'if either of us is delayed,' 'if we get separated in the mall, here's what we'll do...'

8. Put brain in gear before opening mouth. Before saying anything, ask yourself if what you are about to say is 1) True, 2) Kind, and 3) Necessary.

9. Stop worrying, if something concerns you, do something about it. If you can't do anything about it, let it go.

10. For every one thing that goes wrong, there are 50 to 100 blessings. Count them.

11. Learn to live one day at a time.

12. Every day, do at least one thing you really enjoy.

13. Don't sweat the small stuff.

14. Laugh!

15. Remember that the best things in life aren't things.

16. Add an ounce of love to everything you do.

17. If an unpleasant task faces you, do it early in the day and get it over with.

18. Do one thing at a time.[59]

So now, incorporate these tips one at a time, and hopefully you will have a more stress-free environment and the opportunity to spend time with the people and things that are most important in your life.

Peace and blessings to you.

Shipwrecked

"A voyaging ship was wrecked during a storm at sea and only two of the men on it were able to swim to a small, desert-like island. The two survivors…, not knowing what else to do, agreed that they had no other recourse but to pray to God. However, to find out whose prayer was more powerful, they agreed to divide the territory between them and stay on opposite sides of the island.

The first thing they prayed for was food. The next morning, the first man saw a fruit-bearing tree on his side of the land, and he was able to eat its fruit. The other man's parcel of land remained barren.

After a week, the first man was lonely and he decided to pray for a wife. The next day, another ship was wrecked, and the only survivor was a woman who swam to his side of the land. On the other side of the island, there was nothing.

Finally, the first man prayed for a ship, so that he and his wife could leave the island. In the morning, he found a ship docked at his side of the island. The first man boarded the ship with his wife and decided to leave the second man on the island. He considered the other man unworthy to receive God's blessings, since none of his prayers had been answered. For all we know, our blessings are not the fruits of our prayers alone, but those of another praying for us.

'As the ship was about to leave, the first man heard a voice from heaven booming, 'Why are you leaving your companion on the island?'

'My blessings are mine alone, since I was the one who prayed for them,' the first man answered. 'His prayers were all unanswered and so he does not deserve anything.'

'You are mistaken!' the voice rebuked him. 'He had only one prayer, which I answered. If not for that, you would not have received any of my blessings.'

'Tell me,' the first man asked the voice, 'what did he pray for that I should owe him anything?'

'He prayed that all your prayers be answered.'

Moral: For all we know, our blessings are not the fruits of our prayers alone, but those of another praying for us."[60]

My prayer for you today is that all your prayers are answered. Be blessed. Have a wonderful day!

Heaven—Who Will Be There?

Allow me to share with you a poem that was sent to me.

I was shocked, confused, bewildered
As I entered Heaven's door,
Not by the beauty of it all,
By the lights or its decor.

But it was the folks in Heaven
Who made me sputter and gasp—
The thieves, the liars, the sinners,
The alcoholics, the trash.

There stood the kid from seventh grade
Who swiped my lunch money twice.
Next to him was my old neighbor
Who never said anything nice.

Herb, who I always thought
Was rotting away in hell,
Was sitting pretty on cloud nine,
Looking incredibly well.

I nudged Jesus, 'What's the deal?
I would love to hear Your take.
How'd all these sinners get up here?
God must've made a mistake.'

'And why is everyone so quiet,
So somber? Give me a clue.'
'Hush, child,' said He. 'They 're all in shock.
No one thought they'd see you.'[61]

Let us judge NOT. God's forgiveness is for EVERYONE!!
May you find forgiveness today.

When Doors Close

Many times in our life's journey, we get discouraged as we see doors closing on us. That should not be the case. In fact, we should take a hint that God is opening another door—one that leads to better and greater possibilities.

We must realize that nothing happens to us that is without permission from God. So when a door closes, He's opening another one for you so that you can fulfill His plan for your life. He has a plan for your life and, while you are alive, you've got to be going about accomplishing His purpose—which doesn't include looking at closed doors.

That thought is emphasized in the following lines.

The Door of Happiness

When one door of happiness closes,
Another opens;
But often we look so long at the closed door
That we do not see the one which has been opened for us.[62]

Don't dwell on the past when things go wrong; Look for the opened doors all around you!

The Ministry of Trials

The state of California is in bloom. Springtime has awakened the seed that lay dormant during the winter months, and we see tender blades shooting forth from the ground. Tree branches that looked lifeless and dead have come alive with green foliage and delicate blossoms. Nature has painted the mountains with pink, yellow, and red. The Antelope Valley with its California Poppy Reserve is, once again, teeming with visitors. Even Freeway 15 along Lake Elsinore has its surrounding mountains dotted with flowers. We stopped one time on our way from San Diego and took some pictures with these yellow blooms.

Even the young trees in my backyard had some precious lessons to share. Last January, when the Southland of California was battered by storms and unusually cold weather, the wooden fence at the back of my property collapsed under the pressure of the winds and rain. With three spans of wooden fence lying on the ground, there was no way for me to stand it up without help. A couple of trees, a pomegranate and a lemon, had been crushed by the fallen fence. I gave up on them and counted them as part of the casualties from the inclement weather.

After about a month, when the weather had warmed up, I had the fence put back in place. I noticed that the lemon and the pomegranate trees were badly bruised and broken but they still had life in them, and I was certain they would survive. So I put some supports around them and carefully nurtured them back to health. When spring came around, these battered trees were the first to put forth leaves. And today they have the most buds and blossoms when compared to the other trees that didn't sustain any damage from the elements. I am cheering for them, and I am almost certain that they will produce the most fruit of all. Those who persevere over hardships and difficulties are the most fruitful and become a real blessing to the world around them.

I then turned my attention to how this applies to the reality of life. Many times, we are badly bruised and beaten up by the events and circumstances of life. Then we are tempted to give up, thinking that there's no way we can reach our goals or even realize our potential. But those who persevere find that the hardships and difficulties they have experienced help develop their characters and shape a philosophy that can carry them to the pinnacle of success. In the end, these are the people who are the most fruitful and become a real blessing to the world around them.

A proverb reminds us that a bow that is bent to its limits launches its arrow the farthest. In the Bible, Paul says this in his letter to the Corinthian believers: "How that in a great trial of affliction the abundance of their joy and their deep poverty abounded unto the riches of their liberality" (2 Cor. 8:2).

May the trials and hardships we experience in life help us produce abundant fruit of the graces of the Spirit for the glory of God and the blessing of our fellow men.

"My Word...Shall Not Return to Me Void"
(Isa. 55:11)

It's nice to be back from a two-week visit to the Philippines. We had the opportunity of being with family and friends again whom we hadn't seen for a while. It was also special in that we had the chance to be with the new believers for whom we had volunteered to be spiritual guardians. They were doing very well and were growing spiritually and in numbers. The last Sabbath that we were there, I had the privilege of baptizing ten precious souls as a result of the work of the holy Spirit through the efforts of our brethren there.

Five years ago, there was no Seventh-day Adventist church in the village (at La Rioja, Patnongon, Antique) in the Philippines. We decided an Adventist presence should be established there and so we planned to hold an evangelistic campaign. We hired two lay preachers to prepare the ground. When we arrived there nine months later for the series of reaping meetings we have planned, there were no interests that had been prepared by the lay evangelists. They told us they were still in the process of making friends and trying to break the prejudice of the village folk—the place being a strong and closed Catholic enclave.

Needless to say, we were very disappointed. Nevertheless, we went on to hold a two-week evangelistic series of meetings. It was no longer a reaping series of meetings as we have planned. We converted it to a sowing series instead. At the end of the meetings, I didn't ask for baptism, knowing it would not be fair to ask anyone to join the church in so short a time. But we asked for decisions for Christ and for those who wanted to continue to learn more of Him and the church. Several young people and adults signed up and committed to learn more of Christ and His truth.

Since then, a group of believers has been formed, which has been organized into a church. Seven lay evangelists have come and gone. A beautiful chapel and children's center have been built and another building to accommodate an overflow crowd is under construction. The Lord has certainly blessed the work in that heretofore center of Catholicism.

And so, we praise Him who has proven Himself true to His Word. He has promised: "As the rain and the snow come down from heaven, and do not return to it without watering the earth and making it bud and flourish, so that it yields seed for the sower and bread for the eater, so is my word that goes out from my mouth: It will not return to me empty, but will accomplish what I desire and achieve the purpose for which I sent it (Isa. 55:10–11, NIV).

The King Who Was Obedient

"In the eleventh century, King Henry III of Bavaria grew tired of court life and the pressures of being a monarch. He made an application to Prior Richard at a local monastery, asking to be accepted as a contemplative and spend the rest of his life in the monastery.

'Your Majesty,' said Prior Richard, 'do you understand that the pledge here is one of obedience? That will be hard because you have been a king.'

'I understand,' said Henry. 'The rest of my life I will be obedient to you, as Christ leads you.'

'Then I will tell you what to do,' said Prior Richard. 'Go back to your throne and serve faithfully in the place where God has put you.'

When King Henry died, a statement was written: 'The king learned to rule by being obedient.'"[63]

There are times when we get tired of our roles and responsibilities, and life becomes a drag. During these times, it helps to remember that God has planted us in a certain place and has commissioned us to be a good clerk, businessman, accountant, teacher, mother, or father. Christ expects us to be obedient and faithful where He puts us, and, when He returns, He will say to us, "Well done, good and faithful servant; you were faithful over a few things, I will make you ruler over many things"(Matthew 25:21, NKJV).

Blessings Missed

Life is full of opportunities and blessings, but it has its perils and dangers, too. There are open doors, and there are closed doors, as well as pitfalls and favorable moments. As a result, one needs to make wise and informed decisions about what course of action to take in order to succeed.

Some take life by the horns to get their rewards. Others do the same thing, but, for some reason, they fail. Still others take no action for fear that the timing may be wrong or that they may not be properly equipped for the challenge of the hour. And so they sit and do nothing while life passes them by.

Down the road, when this last group people come to the end of their days, they look back and lament the fact that they haven't taken the chances life brought to them because of their fear of failure. They regret the things they haven't done and the opportunities they have missed. It was National Hockey League player Wayne Gretzky, who said, "You miss 100% of the shots you don't take."[64]

The following poem says it more succinctly, albeit in a more humorous way.

There was a very cautious man
Who never laughed or played;
He never risked, he never tried,
He never sang or prayed.

And when he one day passed away
His insurance was denied;
For since he never really lived,
They claimed he never died![65]

The Preacher in Ecclesiastes says, "Rejoice, O young man, in thy youth; and let thy heart cheer thee in the days of thy youth, and walk in the ways of thine heart, and in the sight of thine eyes: but know thou, that for all these things God will bring thee into judgment" (Eccles. 11:9).

To really live, we must grab life by the horns. We must attempt the impossible. We must take risks and not spend the remainder of our days lamenting and wondering what might have been. If we tried something and failed, we won't regret that much because, in the end, we know we tried. And if we succeeded, we can only savor life's sweetness.

That's living!

Rust Out or Wear Out?

A study was done by Harvard University on health and longevity. "The study involved two groups of Harvard graduates between the ages of sixty-five and seventy-five. One group of 100 men retired at sixty-five, and the other group of 100 continued to work to age seventy-five.

In the first group, those who retired at sixty-five, seven out of eight were dead by age seventy-five. In the second group, men who continued to work, only one in seven had died. The conclusion drawn by this study was that retiring too early in life significantly reduces one's probability of surviving that additional 10 years (or more) by a factor of six!"[66] The results are a warning to those whose purpose in retirement is a life of ease and pleasure.

This study shows that we die sooner when we are not doing anything than when we are busy volunteering or engaged in some type of employment. And so, we are given a choice. Would we rather rust out or wear out?

We live longer when we are active, busy, and working to accomplish God's purpose for our lives. The Scriptures say, "By the sweat of your brow you will eat your food until you return to the ground; since from it you were taken; for dust you are and to dust you will return" (Gen. 3:19, NIV). His outline for our lives is that we ought to be working or busily engaged until we are able to or until we go to the grave!

We will all go there if time continues and the Lord doesn't come yet. But there are ways to extend our lives and postpone our appointment with death so that we can accomplish more for the Lord and continue to be a blessing to others while we live.

Worshiping God or Flattering the King?

One of the most impressive places of worship that we visited during our last tour in Europe a few years ago was the chapel in Paris that had been built especially for the kings of France and their royal court. It was an ornate structure that contained all kinds of stained glass windows depicting characters and scenes from the Scriptures. This building was attached to the palace, and it had a secret passageway that led to the king's chamber so the king could enter to worship directly from his bedchamber.

"François Fénelon was the court preacher for King Louis XIV of France in the 17th century. One Sunday when the king and his attendants arrived at the chapel for the regular service, no one else was there but the preacher.

King Louis demanded, 'What does this mean?'

Fenelon replied, "I had published that you would not come to church today, in order that your Majesty might see who serves God in truth and who flatters the king.'"[67]

This was a preacher who had the courage to risk losing his head just to be able to find out the truth about people's church habits. This is still true. A lot of people go to church to see and be seen by others. Some go to church to visit a friend or a relative, while others are there to watch or display their latest fashionable acquisitions.

Worship is not about people or even about us. It is all about God. It is not even about focusing your total energies so that you can find a blessing from the sermon or the music from the choir. It is realizing that the reason you are in there—or the reason we even live—is to worship Him and then to actually do just that. "Therefore, whether you eat or drink, or whatever you do, do all to the glory of God" (1 Cor. 10:31, NKJV).

So let's worship Him—and Him only—every moment of our lives, in a sanctuary built for worship or anywhere we find ourselves to be: for the reason we live is to worship Him.

Trees in the Summer Heat

It's nice to be back after about a month of vacation. The Lord has been good, and we had fun as we traveled and enjoyed the beauty of the Islands. Thanks to those who held us up in their prayers.

One of the things that kept showing up on my electronic news screen while in the Philippines was the heat wave that hit California time and time again. I thought often about my fruit trees that I have been taking care of for the last two years. I would water them nearly every day and put mulch around them now and then to help them to grow. But because there had been no rain and a heat wave in California, I just thought there was no chance that they would still be alive by the time we got back.

When we arrived Monday evening, I peered through the darkness and, by the light of the moon, I noticed the silhouette of the trees that had survived the onslaught of the summer heat.

In the morning, I saw that most of the potted plants had died; they had withered, and the soil in their pots had almost turned to rock. Trees that were planted in the ground had survived, although some of their tender tops have become crispy and had dried up. Some of the succulents had been able to live off the food and water stored up in their systems. Banana trees that were four inches in diameter had decreased to half that size, and the cactus plants that were thick and plump had become thin and hard. Other plants were helped by the fact that they were planted in an area where they had some shade from the burning heat of the sun, and they didn't show any sign of distress.

Then I thought about our spiritual lives, and how it will be during the time of trouble. Like the potted plants that are unable to survive the heat waves of summer, believers who have no direct connection with Jesus as their Lord and Savior are not going to make it. It is not enough to depend on a faith that has been borrowed from one's parents, elders, or other spiritual leaders. One has to have his or her own personal relationship with the Lord in order to survive and have roots that go down deep into the soil of His grace.

Ellen White wrote, "None but those who have fortified the mind with the truths of the Bible will stand through the last great conflict."[68] Like succulents, we can survive the crisis ahead by making preparations now and fortifying our minds with the truths of the Scriptures. And, of course, those who put their faith in the cross of Jesus will be sheltered from the storm and will find a refuge, "...as the shadow of a great rock in a weary land" (Isa. 32:2).

Let us each one of us strive to "...be like a tree planted by the rivers of water, that brings forth its fruit in its season, whose leaf also shall not wither..." (Ps. 1:3, NKJV).

Ten Signs That Show You Could Live to Be a Hundred

Early in the year, we lost a centenarian at our church. A few more of our members will reach the century mark in a short while. In 2014 in the United States, there were more than 72,000 of this age, which is a forty-four percent increase since 2000.[69] In 2018, *Reader's Digest* published an article that gave some signs that tell if you would be a good candidate for this elite group.[70] They include the following.

1. You don't feel your age. You may be sixty, but you're feeling as if you're fifty or fifty-five. Studies show that those who felt three or four years younger than their age were less likely to die over an eight-year period than those who felt their age or older. On the other hand, feeling older was linked to a forty-one percent risk of dying.

2. You love eating fruits and veggies. A University of Michigan study of 700 women in their seventies showed that those who consumed the most veggies and fruit had a forty-six percent lower chance of dying over a five-year period compared with those who ate them infrequently. Okinawa, Japan has the most centenarians in the world (ratio-wise), because older Okinawans have eaten a plant-based diet most of their lives and almost all grow or once grew a garden.

3. You are joyful and optimistic, relatively free from worries and anxiety. In a 2012 study of 243 volunteers published in the journal *Aging*, nearcentenarians share some common characteristics and personality traits. Rosanne Leipzig, MD, PhD, professor of geriatrics and palliative medicine at the Icahn School of Medicine at Mount Sinai in New York City says, "being adaptable and flexible helps people avoid stress and anxiety, which can increase longevity."

4. You eat a lot of fish. A Harvard study found that older adults with the highest blood levels of omega-3 fatty acids lived two

more years, on average, than those with lower blood levels. They didn't take fish oil supplements. They simply ate a lot of fish, which is packed with omega-3s.

5. You eat Greek-ish. A Mediterranean-style diet that emphasizes olive oil, legumes, nuts, and whole grains, as well as fruits, veggies, and fish has been linked to long life. Harvard researchers studied 4,600 women and found that those who closely followed this style of eating had the least cellular aging.

6. You take regular afternoon naps. Ikaria, Greece, is a small island in the Mediterranean that has a high population of centenarians. Residents are fond of an afternoon nap and Harvard researchers have studied 23,000 people for six years and found that those who regularly took a thirty-minute siesta had a thirty-seven percent lower chance of dying from heart disease than did those who stayed awake all day.

7. You remain active: walk, run, bike, jog, or do other sports activities. A 2012 study in *Archives of Internal Medicine* confirmed that those who were the most fit among 19,000 middle-aged adults were less likely to develop Alzheimer's disease, certain cancers, heart disease, and type 2 diabetes in their seventies and beyond. "People who remain active throughout their life span, whether that's running, walking, or riding bikes, live longer," says Jeremy Walston, MD, a professor of geriatric medicine at Johns Hopkins University School of Medicine.

8. You have a sense of purpose in life. A new study in *Psychological Science* found that people who feel they have a sense of purpose in life are less likely to die over a fourteen-year period. "Make a new friend, pick up a new hobby, or volunteer", says Dr. Leipzig. "My great uncle, who is in his mid-90's, still worked in his woodshop almost every day," adds Dr. Walston.

9. You've got a shorter waistline. You've heard it before, "The longer the waistline, the shorter the lifeline." Women with a waist of thirty-seven inches or more had a life expectancy that was five years lower after age forty than did women with a waist of twenty-seven inches or less, according to one study.

For men, a waist of forty-three inches or more was linked to a three-year decrease in life expectancy compared with those with a waist of thirty-five inches or less. Trimming a few inches from your pants' size may have a powerful health impact. "I tell my patients that whenever possible, walk, don't drive," says Dr. Leipzig.

10. You're connected to family and friends. Feeling connected to family and friends keeps people engaged, and that facilitates healthy aging, says Dr. Walston. "Being isolated works in the other direction and can lead to chronic illnesses." In Sardinia, Italy, a tiny Mediterranean island with a large centenarian population, friendship is key, according to Dan Buettner, a National Geographic fellow who has traveled the world to study its longest-living people. "Life is very social. People meet on the street daily and savor each other's company. They count on each other. If a neighbor gets sick, a neighbor is right there," he wrote in the *Wall Street Journal*.

There we have them all! Let us strive to live like these people who are among the longest-living people on the face of the earth. Jesus has not only promised us eternal life—which is the best gift we can ever have—but He also wants to give us abundant life in the here and now (John 10:10). To accept His gift of health and long life in the here and now is to really appreciate His best plans and love for all of us.

The Ant and the Leaf

"One Sunday morning, a wealthy man sat on his balcony enjoying sunshine…when a little ant caught his eye which was going from one side to the other side of the balcony carrying a big leaf several times more than its size. The man watched it for more than an hour. He saw that the ant faced many impediments during its journey, paused, took a diversion and then continued towards its destination. The man was captivated by the ant, one of God's tiniest creatures. Its abilities to analyze and reason showed the greatness of the Creator.

At one point, the tiny creature came across a crack in the floor. It paused for a little while, analyzed, and then laid the huge leaf over the crack, walked over the leaf, picked up the leaf on the other side, then continued its journey. The man was captivated by the cleverness of the ant, one of God's tiniest creatures.

The incident left the man in awe and forced him to contemplate the miracle of Creation. It showed the greatness of the Creator. In front of his eyes, there was this tiny creature of God, lacking in size yet equipped with a brain to analyze, contemplate, reason, explore, discover, and overcome. Along with all these capabilities, the man also noticed that this tiny creature shared some human shortcomings.

The man saw about an hour later that the creature had reached its destination—a tiny hole in the floor which was the entrance to its underground dwelling. And it was at this point that the ant's shortcoming, that it shared with the man, was revealed. How could the ant carry into the tiny hole the large leaf that it had managed to carefully bring to the destination? It simply couldn't! So the tiny creature—after all the painstaking, hard work and exercising great skills by overcoming all the

> *The man was captivated by the ant, one of God's tiniest creatures. Its abilities to analyze and reason showed the greatness of the Creator.*

difficulties along the way—just left behind the large leaf and went home empty-handed.

The ant had not thought about the end before it began its challenging journey and, in the end, the large leaf was nothing more than a burden to it. The creature had no option but to leave it behind to reach its destination. The man learned a great lesson that day.

Isn't that the truth about our lives? We worry about our family, we worry about our job, we worry about how to earn more money, we worry about where we should live—all sorts of things, only to abandon all these things when we reach our destination—the grave."[71]

In our life's journey these are simply heavy burdens that we carry with so much care and difficulty, only to find that, at the end, they are meaningless and useless because we can't take them to heaven with us.

This is just like Jesus's parable of the rich fool. The man said to himself, "Soul, thou hast much goods laid up for many years; take thine ease, eat, drink, and be merry. But God said unto him, Thou fool, this night thy soul shall be required of thee: then whose shall those things be, which thou hast provided" (Luke 12:19–20).

The Greatest Hazard in Life

Someone has said that life is just a gamble. What is meant is that, in life, sometimes we win and sometimes we lose. The idea is to live our lives so that we come out winners and not losers. This is because life is a precious gift which we receive from God. But we still must choose to receive it and show our appreciation for this blessing by enjoying it to its fullest in spite of the risks that come with it.

Others, however, in an attempt to avoid losing, never try or attempt anything at all. But that is more tragic, because it guarantees the loss.

William Arthur Ward penned it this way in his poem "Risk":

To laugh is to risk appearing a fool.
To weep is to risk appearing sentimental.
To reach out to another is to risk involvement.
To expose feelings is to risk exposing your true self.
To place your ideas and dreams before a crowd is to risk their loss.
To love is to risk not being loved in return.
To hope is to risk despair.
To try is to risk failure.
But risks must be taken, because the greatest hazard in life is to risk nothing.[72]

So go ahead. Laugh, weep, try, hope, and reach out and love someone. You will risk pain, failure, and loss, but the greatest of all hazards in life is to have risked nothing. And to have never risked anything is to have never lived at all.

The Mountain Man[73]

For years, he was called a madman for toiling away on the rocks. But Dashrath Manjhi was not crazy. His quest to break a path through a small mountain to benefit his entire village is now legendary because he carved an entire road with hand tools, working for twenty-two years.

Manjhi started off his extraordinary task in 1960, after his wife was injured while trekking up the side of one of the rocky footpaths. To get to the nearest hospital, he had to travel around the mountains, a distance of some seventy kilometers. She died as they were not able to reach the doctors in time to save her.

Dashrath Manjhi wanted his people to have easier access to doctors, schools, and opportunity. Armed with only a sledge hammer, chisel, and crowbar, he single-handedly began carving a road through the 300-foot mountain that isolated his village from the nearest town.

He sold the family's three goats to buy the hammer and chisels and worked every day on the project to make it successful. After plowing fields for others in the morning, he would work on his road all evening and throughout the night.

After twenty-two years, Dashrath Manjhi had broken the mountain: he had carved out a road 360 feet long and thirty feet wide. Wazirganj, with its doctors, jobs, and school, was now only five kilometers away. People from sixty villages in Atri could use his road.

The health of his village is owed to the man who carved through a mountain, Dashrath Manjhi who did something so that the tragedy that he experienced in his life would not be felt by any other man. He didn't have heavy-duty machines to do the herculean task, but he found a way to do it by using crude and simple tools, with his blood, sweat, and tears and by earning his living during the day and toiling on the mountain in the night.

He was mocked and ridiculed as a mad man, but his vision, his determination and grit, his commitment to this goal, and his love for people who wouldn't care, earned him the success that he coveted. In the end, he was recognized for his achievement and hundreds of people from his village and the outlying areas were eternally grateful to him for their easy access to education, health care, and the very preservation of their lives.

Manjhi's story reminds us that Jesus did even more than this for us. Jesus was rich and yet He became poor so that, through his poverty, we may be made rich. And he endured everything, even death on the cross for people who didn't care. "He came unto his own, and his own received him not" (John 1:11). But He endured it all because of the joy that was set before Him, the joy of seeing people eternally saved in the kingdom because of His sacrifice (Heb. 12:2).

The Master's Touch

Too often, we give up on someone and, in exasperation, say, "He is a hopeless case. He is messed up, and there's no way he can turn around. Nothing can be done to make him change for the better."

But, in doing so, we underestimate the power of God. The apostle Paul says: "For I am not ashamed of the gospel of Christ: for it is the power of God unto salvation to every one that believeth; to the Jew first, and also to the Greek" (Rom.1:16).

When we think we have done everything we can to help someone turn around and make something out of his or her life, but still we see no positive results, we should not give up. It is at this point that we need to let go and let God.[74] And we will find that, with God, there is nothing impossible. Truly, with Him, the difficult is easy, and the impossible? …just needs a little more time.

The following material states this point beautifully. No matter how messed up and dysfunctional our lives may be, if we give our lives to Him, He will touch us and—with the skill of the Master's hands—He will help us produce a melody that will sweeten and brighten the world we live in.

The Touch

"It was battered and scarred, and the auctioneer thought it scarcely worth his while to waste much time on the old violin. But he held it up with a smile.

'What am I bidden good folks,' he cried. 'Who'll start the bidding for me? A dollar; a dollar. Then two! Only two? Two dollars, and who'll make it three? Three dollars once, three dollars twice; going for three…' But no.

From the room, far back, a gray-haired man came forward and picked up the bow. Then, wiping the dust from the old violin, and tightening the loose strings, he played a melody pure and sweet as a caroling angel sings….

And many a man with life out of tune, and battered and scarred with sin, is auctioned cheap to the thoughtless crowd, much like the old violin. 'A mess of pottage,' a glass of wine, a game—and he travels on. He is 'going' once, and 'going' twice, he's 'going' and almost 'gone.'

But the Master comes, and the foolish crowd never can quite understand the worth of a soul', and the change that is wrought by the touch of the Master's Hand."[75]

May we all with gracious understanding and patience wait on those whom God is touching with the skill of His hands, knowing that we too— to a certain degree— are undergoing a similar process of restorative work. And, better still, may we be instruments in His hands to help shape and mold others for His glory.

The Woodcutter

In his book, *The 7 Habits of Highly Effective People*, Steven Covey tells the story of the woodcutter.

"A very strong woodcutter asked for a job in a timber company and he got it. The pay was really good and so were the working conditions. For those reasons, the woodcutter was determined to do his best.

His boss gave him an axe and showed him the area where he was supposed to work.

The first day, the woodcutter brought in eighteen trees.

'Congratulations,' the boss said. 'Go on that way!'

Very motivated by the boss's words, the woodcutter tried harder the next day, but he could only bring fifteen trees. The third day he tried even harder, but he could only bring ten trees. Day after day he was bringing less and less trees.

'I must be losing my strength,' the woodcutter thought. He went to the boss and apologized, saying that he could not understand what was going on.

'When was the last time you sharpened your axe?' the boss asked.

'Sharpen? I had no time to sharpen my axe. I have been very busy trying to cut trees.'"[76]

> *The act of the Holy Spirit in renewing and sharpening us needs to happen on a regular basis.*

The act of the Holy Spirit in renewing and sharpening us needs to happen on a regular basis.

Our lives are just like that. In today's world, everyone is busier than ever, but less happy than ever. We need to take time to sharpen the "axe." If we don't, we will become dull and lose our effectiveness. There is nothing wrong with activity and hard work, but we should not get so busy that we neglect the truly important things in life—like our personal life, taking time to get close to our Creator, giving more time for our family, or taking time to read etc.

We can sharpen the "axe" of our physical and mental lives by making sure we have good nutrition, proper rest, regular exercise, and the right amount of air, water, and sunshine.

And for our spiritual life, Paul says in his letter to the Romans that we should be transformed by the renewing of our minds (Rom. 12:2) through the regenerating power of the Holy Spirit.

This act of the Holy Spirit in renewing and sharpening us needs to happen on a regular basis. In fact Ellen G. White talks about it when she says we need to "Consecrate yourself to God every morning; make this your very first work"[77] every day.

Thus we may be able to sharpen the "axe," so that we can be effective woodcutters for God in the advancement of His kingdom.

Things Closest to Us

Rains had kept us indoors for much of the past two weeks, and so, when the sun comes up, we usually see it as a chance to play some tennis or golf. This time though, I decided to go to my backyard late in the afternoon and tend the fruit trees that I planted there two years ago. It was also a time to repair the dirt steps that I had built for easier access to our hillside garden.

I must have enjoyed flexing my muscles without pausing from the work I was doing so that, after about two hours, I looked to the west and my eyes were greeted by a spectacular sight. A glorious sunset presented itself right before my very eyes. I was so delighted by this beautiful scene, which I had not witnessed before from that section of our property. I stopped for a moment to thank God for such beauty and for eyes that were able to see and appreciate these things.

As I continued to dwell on this wondrous sight, another thought crossed my mind. It struck me that there are many things around us that are so grand and so majestic, and yet we have not noticed them simply because we haven't taken the time to slow down and open our eyes to them. We travel to distant lands and spend lots of money in search of beautiful things to gaze at and wonder upon. But many of these beautiful things are just right around us, if we know where to look and if we slow down and take the time to appreciate them.

So, let us slow down, open our eyes, and look and see and appreciate such things that God has placed before our very eyes. He is trying to reach us at every moment, and so let us be sensitive to His messages.

Just Trust His Heart

Many times, we don't recognize God's answer to our prayers just because it does not come in the package we anticipated or in the size and shape we asked for. This happens because we do not know what is best for us and are unaware of our greatest need. God, who knows everything about us and who loves us as a father cherishes his children, gives to us—not according to our desires—but according to what He sees is best for us. Thus the need to simply trust in God.

God also wants to work with us. He want us to partner with Him, even in our work of character development. He sometimes allows us to experience certain things that are difficult and tough if He knows that they will help in refining and perfecting our characters.

In the end, we will see and understand why God did certain things, and we will recognize that God was right after all and that—all the time—He was making sure that we obtained the greatest and the best.

Jesus asks in Matthew 7:9–11, "Which of you, if your son asks for bread, will give him a stone? Or if he asks for a fish, will give him a snake? If you, then, though you are evil, know how to give good gifts to your children, how much more will your Father in heaven give good gifts to hose who ask him!" (NIV).

Trust in God. You may not receive the things that you desired or wanted in the first place, but you will be satisfied because these are all that you needed, fresh from the hands of God.

When It's Time to Change Your Life

We work to earn a living and support a family. Some people may not have to if they have inherited wealth that takes care of their needs for life. Others stop working after the children are grown and are out on their own. And when sufficient funds have been accumulated to assure a comfortable life through the golden years, what is there to work for?

Of course, when one is in good health and considers work as a service to God and fellowman, it is altogether different. One can stay on the job for as long as he or she is still productive and useful.

Somewhere down the road though, things stop being exciting. Every day is a grind, and work becomes a drudgery. There is no looking forward with eagerness and anticipation to the workday.

Someone did research and came up with some signs can tell you when it's time for a change. When conditions— such as mentioned below— exist, you know there's no more future in your job, and every additional day that you stay is a waste of time. The time has come to change your life. Are you familiar with the following?

"1. You dread going to work more days than you don't.

2. You are living in the past or dreaming about the future.

3. People are constantly telling you to relax.

4. You are jealous of other people's successes.

5. You wake up tired."[78]

6. You are antsy.

7. You gossip.

8. Everyone seems to annoy you.

9. You have a constant sense of foreboding.

10. You are always thinking and are deep in thought all the time.

Having the courage to stop and change direction at this point in your life will pay you dividends in terms of your health and happiness. It will be a struggle. You may have to start all over again. It will be an uphill climb, but you will make it with determination and perseverance. In the end, you will find yourself in a better, healthier, and more meaningful world.

Whatever you do, do it as though you are doing it for the Lord, and you'll never go wrong. Paul admonishes that we ought to be concerned—not with men's approval—but with God's. "But as we were allowed of God to be put in trust with the gospel, even so we speak; not as pleasing men, but God, which trieth our hearts" (1 Thess. 2:4).

When Life Breaks Down

In the beginning, God created the earth and then made man in His own image. "Man was to bear God's image, both in outward resemblance and in character.... Adam's height was much greater than that of men who now inhabit the earth. Eve was somewhat less in stature; yet her form was noble and full of beauty...They were full of vigor imparted by the tree of life, and their intellectual power was but a little less than that of the angels.[79]

When your car breaks down, you know you probably can't fix it yourself, and so you take it to an experienced auto mechanic who can find out what the problem is and has the knowledge and the tools to fix it.

> *When your life breaks down, don't ever think that you know how to fix everything.*

When your life breaks down, don't ever think that you know how to fix everything...that you don't need any help. Always remember, only God knows how to fix our lives because we are His creation, and He loves us so much.

Even when life seems to have lost its meaning and we are facing a blank wall or think we have reached the end of our road, He invites us to just come to Him. He says, "Come unto me, all ye that labour and are heavy laden, and I will give you rest. Take my yoke upon you and learn of me; for I am meek and lowly in heart: and ye shall find rest unto your souls" (Matt. 11:28–30).

Why I Stay Away from Church

A pastor wrote about why he stopped attending athletic events. In so doing, he created a scenario using his love-hate relationship with sports as an illustration of why some people stay away from church.

"Every time I went, they asked me for money.

The people with whom I had to sit didn't seem very friendly.

The seats were too hard and not comfortable.

The coach never came to call on me.

The referee made a decision with which I could not agree.

I was sitting with some hypocrites—they came only to see what others were wearing.

Some games went into overtime, and I was late getting home.

The band played some numbers that I had never heard before.

The games are scheduled when I want to do other things.

My parents took me to too many games when I was growing up....

I don't want to take my children because I want them to choose for themselves what sport they like best."[80]

You may have realized by now that the above excuses the person has for no longer attending sporting events is a hypothetical situation he created that has the same reasons some people give for no longer attending church. But do you see how these seem so absurd and ridiculous?

If one is a sports fan(atic), weather conditions are hardly a factor. And physical and social inconveniences can never stop a fan from going to a game, enjoying it, and supporting and cheering for his favorite sports team. And so it is with one whose heart is committed to Jesus. None of the inconveniences or imperfections that may surround the activity can stop him from going to God's house, enjoying His presence, and meeting with His people.

The writer of the book of Hebrews says, "Not forsaking the assembling of ourselves together, as the manner of some is; but exhorting one another: and so much the more, as ye see the day approaching" (Heb. 10:25).

May our experience be just like that of David's when he said, "I was glad when they said unto me, Let us go into the house of the Lord" (Ps. 122:1).

Hands Uplifted for an Open Mind

We know much about how the mind influences the body but not so much about how the body influences the mind.

Researchers call this phenomenon *embodied cognition*[81] in which the brain takes mental cues from physical gestures. It's similar to when we offer someone a helping hand, ask for help, or prepare to receive something—in each example, our palms are upturned; and when we reject something or push someone away, our palms are face down.

Further examples of this are the positions we take in prayer. Kneeling down or reverently bowing the head sends a message of humiliation and worship to the brain. Putting the hands up cues the mind for praise, and extending the hands out with open palms readies the mind to receive the blessings that are being asked for.

In the case of feeding the 5,000 with the five loaves and two fishes (Matt. 14:17–21), Jesus told the disciples to make the multitudes sit down. The people sat down in obedience to the instructions from the Lord. It showed their faith in Jesus's ability to feed them and fill them up despite the meager provisions. By sitting down, the people gave a message to their brains that there was food that was going to be served, and Jesus rewarded their faith in His power to provide.

Contented or Covetous?

"In the fifth century, a man named Arenius determined to live a holy life. So he abandoned the comforts of Egyptian society to follow an austere lifestyle in the desert. Yet whenever he visited the great city of Alexandria, he spent time wandering through its bazaars. When asked why, he explained that his heart rejoiced at the sight of all the things he didn't need."[82]

Arenius found happiness in visiting the shops, not because he delighted in the sight of all the trinkets of civilization but because it made him ecstatic to realize that there were so many things that he didn't need anymore—things he could live without.

Our typical supermarkets today carry as many as 40,000 to 50,000 items.[83] But how many of these are absolutely essential? And how many are unnecessary? Going window shopping or visiting the mall may either be beneficial or a waste of time depending on the purpose. Other than the beneficial exercise that one gets by walking around for some length of time, looking at all the displays of the latest trends in fashion and gadgets simply creates a spirit of covetousness or discontent. It develops in us a desire to possess something with a high price tag that could lead us to having to work an excessive number of hours or take on another shift. That's why the tenth commandment warns us against covetousness of things or persons (Exod. 20:17).

But if you take something that has the potential for evil, and then you sublimate it by mentally assigning a higher, more noble purpose for it, then—like Arenius—you can go to the shops and grow your contented spirit by looking at all the toys and gadgets on display and then congratulating yourself for reigning in your desires and having the creativity, ingenuity, and contentment (with what you already have) that you can still enjoy life to its fullest without these crutches.

So, the next time you find yourself on a trip to the mall, ask yourself this question: Am I going to rejoice at the sight of things that I see I don't really need, or am I going there to give in to the spirit of covetousness that will lead to the ruin of my soul? The choice is yours now, but the consequences are eternal!

Most Dangerous Times for the Heart

No doubt the heart is one of the most vital organs of the body. As the heart goes, so does the body. When the heart gives out, so does everything. When the heart is healthy, the body can be healthy.

For so long now, World Health Organization statistics have continued to show that heart disease is the number one cause of death in the United States and throughout the world. So it is important to take care of this vital part of the body.

Joel K. Kahn, MD, Clinical Professor of Medicine at Wayne State University and Director of Cardiac Wellness at Michigan Healthcare Professionals PC, mentions certain predictable "danger zones,"[84] especially for individuals with heart disease or at risk for heart disease because of smoking, diabetes, high cholesterol, or high blood pressure. They are the following.

1. Death of a loved one. Research shows those grieving the loss of a loved one have an increased risk of a heart attack the week following the loss; and, in Sweden, studies indicate that the risk of a heart attack remains elevated for several years following the death of an adult sibling. So when this event happens, don't sit alone and suffer. Seek counseling and support from friends and family.

2. A bout of the flu. Odds of a heart attack quadruple 3 days following this illness. The virus triggers an inflammatory response that can damage arteries, and dehydration thickens the blood, making it prone to clot. The fever can also increase the heart rate, forcing the heart to work harder.

3. A devastating natural disaster. Three weeks after an 8.9 magnitude earthquake and accompanying tsunami killed thousands in Japan in 2011, the rate of heart attacks among survivors increased threefold compared with the rate during the same calendar weeks in previous years.

4. A big sporting event. Even cheering for your team can break

your heart if you allow your emotions to spiral out of control. In Brazil, where soccer's World Cup is serious business, data from four Cups show that heart attacks increased during the tournament's finals and they were highest when Brazil was playing, compared to other teams.

5. A manic Monday. Research shows that heart attacks happen when we return to work after a break. Stress over the coming workweek raises the level of adrenalin and cortisol, which may increase blood pressure and blood clotting. Starting the week on a calmer note—along with prayer and meditation and walking at lunch to relieve midday stress—are some good things to include in one's routine.

6. Shoveling snow. Cold weather and heavy labor put a tremendous stress on the heart. Researchers described heart attacks that occurred in patients who suffered a clot in a previously placed stent during or soon after shoveling snow. Dressing warmly, taking frequent breaks, and staying hydrated are good ways of preventing a heart attack. Or better yet, let someone else do the shoveling.

In the spiritual realm, heart is also used to describe the mind, the vital part of the human body through which God interacts with us and communicates His will. He admonishes us to particularly guard it because our total spiritual well-being depends on it. Proverbs 4:23 says: "Keep thy heart with all diligence; for out of it are the issues of life."

Diet, Fatigue, and Sleeping Difficulties

In an Australian study, "it was discovered that men with high-fat diets were more likely to suffer from daytime fatigue and poor night-time slumber than men with low-fat diets…. Scientists speculated that fat intake affects hormones, metabolism, and the central nervous system, all of which interact with the circadian clock that regulates shut-eye. In addition, the lead author noted that sleeping poorly makes people crave rich, fatty foods thus creating a vicious cycle."[85]

The Dietary Guidelines for Americans recommends that adults get no more than ten percent of their total calories from fat.[86]

For those who complain of daytime fatigue and difficulty sleeping, do not think it is simply because you are getting old. Cutting down on the fat intake in your diet may take care of these problems. And, of course, trusting in God and resting in His care are what we need to renew our strength and have a good sleep at night.

The Scriptures declare, "It is vain for you to rise up early, to sit up late, to eat the bread of sorrows: for so he gives his beloved sleep" (Ps. 127:2). And again in Isaiah 40:31, the prophets writes, "But they that wait upon the LORD shall renew their strength; they shall mount up with wings as eagles; they shall run, and not be weary; and they shall walk, and not faint" (Isa. 40:31).

To renew our strength and not be weary or fatigued and to be able to sleep in peace and rest, we need to trust in the Lord, wait patiently on Him, and stay away from a high-fat diet.

> *"But they that wait upon the LORD shall renew their strength; they shall mount up with wings as eagles; they shall run, and not be weary; and they shall walk, and not faint" (Isa. 40:31).*

The Fight Against Alzheimer's Disease

Alzheimer's disease is a terrible disease. In its later stages, it's not so much the person's physical pain but the total mental and emotional disconnect from the land of the living that is so tragic and heart rending. Physically the patient is there, but mentally and emotionally, he or she is in another world.

Science and modern medicine still haven't found a cure for Alzheimer's disease. Its progress may be delayed but that's about it, and the best way to deal with this living death is to prevent its onset. Psychiatrist Gary Small, MD, Director of the UCLA Longevity Center, suggests certain important lifestyle changes that could help in the struggle against this disease in his book, *The Alzheimer's Prevention Program: Keep Your Brain Healthy for the Rest of Your Life*.[87] These steps include the following:

1. Exercise. Physical activity not only bulks up arm and leg muscles but key portions of the brain as well.

2. Stretch the mind. Challenge the mind by learning a new hobby or anything new that's interesting. Keep your brain constantly engaged.

3. Feed the brain. Choose foods that are good for the brain. Just don't eat too much because overweight and obese people in midlife have double and quadruple the risk of dementia respectively. Eat the Mediterranean-style diet, which emphasizes vegetables, grains, and fish, lowers the risk of diabetes, which is a major risk factor for Alzheimer's disease.

4. Take supplements. Omega-3 fatty acids, curcumin, and multivitamins have an anti-inflammatory effect and lower the risk of Alzheimer's disease.

5. Connect with family and friends. Studies show that having a network of friends can lower the risk of dementia by as much as sixty percent.

6. Manage your stress. Learn how to relax. Get a massage. Easily stressed people are twice as likely to develop Alzheimer's as compared to calmer people, when studied over a five-year period.

7. Meditate. Researches show that this can actually increase the size of parts of the brain that control memory.

I want to add to this list the factor of SLEEP. Sleep deprivation is known to speed aging of the brain. A study[88] that followed Chinese adults ages fifty-five since 2005 showed how the brain changes in size. As we age, brain tissue shrinks in volume, but the less sleep the participants got, the faster their brains shrunk- and the more steeply their cognition declined. In addition, it is also known that sleep helps remove toxic wastes from the brain[89] and therefore contributes to clarity of thought and greater retention of memory.

So, be sure to get enough hours of sleep. You can delay shrinking of your brain tissues, eliminate toxic wastes from the brain, and fight off Alzheimer's disease.

The Scripture says in 2 Timothy 1:7, "For God hath not given us the spirit of fear; but of power, and of love, and of a sound mind." God gave us a "sound mind." Let us keep it that way because He wants to communicate with us and wants to make this part of our body a living temple—a dwelling place for Him.

Grandparenting to Sharpen the Mind

In an Australian study of 186 older women, it was shown that spending some time caring for grandchildren can keep the mind sharp. Grandmothers who watched their grandchildren one day a week did better on cognitive tests than those who cared for grandchildren more often or not at all.[90]

This study is continuing and researchers are trying to find out the exact reason why this is so, and they are also learning how social engagement affects elders' acuity.

I believe that one of the reasons why is because children are, by nature, very inquisitive. They look at life with a sense of wonder and delight. They ask all kinds of questions. They want to understand. They like to know why things happen a certain way. And when they ask Grandma and Grandpa for answers to their questions, the grandparents' minds are renewed, revitalized, and sharpened.

Those who do not care for their grandchildren did not do as well in their cognitive tests, and this is understandable. Those who cared for their grandchildren five days a week or more did not do as well on tests for mental sharpness. This may be little kids can be a source of mental fatigue and even a plain nuisance—something that negative impacts mood. After all, nature did not plan for grandparents to be rearing little children on a full-time basis, unless this responsibility was thrust upon them by unavoidable circumstances such as death or incapacity on the part of the parents.

My take here would be that we should find time to expose ourselves to youthful minds that look at life with a sense of wonder, and we should welcome the opportunity to help children understand its mysteries and complexities. And most important of all, let us teach them faith in the Creator God who showed us His love by sending His Son to die for us so that we can have life forevermore. This was the case of Timothy whose faith was instilled and developed in him through the patient teachings of his grandmother Lois and his mother Eunice, for which the apostle Paul rejoiced (2 Tim. 1:5).

Honoring Grandparents

Grandparents Day was first celebrated in 1979 when President Jimmy Carter proclaimed the first Sunday following the Labor Day weekend as National Grandparents Day.[91] It was a day set aside to honor grandparents for the role they play in nurturing families, and it was initiated through the efforts of Marian McQuade of West Virginia with the behind-the-scenes support of husband Joseph. They had fifteen children, forty-three grandchildren, ten great grandchildren, and one great-great grandchild.[92]

There are three purposes for National Grandparents Day.

1. To honor grandparents.

2. To give grandparents an opportunity to show love to their children's children.

3. To help children become aware of the strength, information, and guidance that older people can offer.

It's time we saw grandparents as more than glorified babysitters. They serve as surrogate parents who bring love and assure the continuance of the cultural values and spiritual principles that shape and mold the lives of family members and validate their self-worth.

As we take time to honor grandparents, I want to share something my one grandchild said to me that was the greatest tribute a grandparent could receive. While driving by the local Home Depot one morning, we saw an unusual number of men standing at the entrance to the store, who were asking for day jobs from the customers who came to the store. Wanting to take the opportunity to teach a life lesson to my grandkids, I started to tell them of the importance of going to school, of studying hard, and of finishing a course. I said many of those people did not finish school, so they have to come here every day to look for a job. If no one hires them, they go home without any money. Without money, they don't have food on the table. In those circumstances, life can be very hard.

I wasn't prepared for this, but Katelynn, my older grandchild, was deep in thought and she said, "Don't they have grandmas and grandpas?"

What more can I say.

Hurried and Busy or Composed and Relaxed?

"But seek ye first the kingdom of God.... Therefore take no thought for the morrow.... Sufficient unto the day is the evil thereof" (Matt. 6:33–34).

Author Eric Hoffer writes the following:

"The feeling of being hurried is not usually the result of living a full life and having no time. It is, on the contrary, born of a vague fear that we are wasting our life. When we do not do the one thing we ought to do, we have no time for anything else—we are the busiest people in the world."[93]

The above quote makes us better understand the words of Jesus, "But seek ye first the kingdom of God, and His righteousness; and all these things shall be added unto you. Take therefore no thought for the morrow: for the morrow shall take thought for the things of itself. Sufficient unto the day is the evil thereof" (Matt. 6:33–34). And again, in Mark 6:31, Jesus says, "… Come ye yourselves apart into a desert place, and rest a while: for there were many coming and going, and they had no leisure so much as to eat."

> *Knowing what we ought to do and focusing on doing it is the key to a full, unhurried, and contented life.*

Knowing what we ought to do and focusing on doing it is the key to a full, unhurried, and contented life. It is when we are distracted from the main purpose of our lives that we feel the boredom of a meaningless existence, and that is when we have the feeling of being so busy and having no time for anything else.

So let's zero in on what we are here on earth for—which is to focus on and get acquainted with God and to be at peace (Job 22:21)—settled, relaxed, and fulfilled. For knowing Him as the only true God and Jesus Christ whom He has sent (John 17:3) is to have eternal life in heaven and on the earth made new in perfect peace, happiness, and prosperity.

Rocks, Rocks, and More Rocks

Last Sunday, our group of twenty-five members drove 150 miles to the Joshua Tree National Park in Twentynine Palms, California, for a day out in nature. It was a day that was perfect for picnicking, sightseeing, and hiking out in the desert.

We got there shortly before noontime, which was just the right time to spread out the delicacies and goodies on the picnic tables and fill up our hungry stomachs. Then came the hike to Hidden Valley past rocks that took on interesting shapes: a whale, a lion, Snoopy dog, and a few that could pass for the nondescript beast in Daniel's prophetic book.

The weather was just perfect for a day out in the rugged wilderness. In fact, the event almost got canceled due to a forecast of rain, but the weather turned out to be perfect after all. The sun shone from a clear blue sky with white clouds above, but it was kind of chilly, which was just the right combination for a leisurely hike.

It was a memorable day—a day to experience renewal and strengthening of fellowship ties. The awesome rock formations and spectacular natural wonders also gave witness to the majesty and artistic mind of God, who carved these rock specimens with His wind, rain, and sun.

I was reading Psalm 61, and the psalmist says in verse 2: "From the ends of the earth I will call to you, I call as my heart grows faint; lead me to the rock that is higher than I" (NIV).

As we drove around this huge natural preserve and during the hike, we saw a number of rock climbers; some were busy scaling the imposing walls, while a few others had successfully reached the top of the rock, their goal achieved. The psalmist, however, asks to be led to the Rock that is higher than he. This Rock is Jesus. And getting on this Rock not only spells achievement and success but also euphoria and exhilaration. It also means being safe in His arms, away from and unreached by the evil and trouble that sweep the earth.

Let us, with David, pray that we may be led to the Rock that is higher than us. Then will we have peace, and joy and safety from the troubles of this old and sinful world.

Khrushchev and the Bible

"At the village church in Kalinovka, Russia, attendance at Sunday school picked up after the priest started handing out candy to the peasant children. One of the most faithful was a pug-nosed, pugnacious lad who recited his Scriptures with proper piety, pocketed his reward, then fled into the fields to munch on it.

The priest took a liking to the boy, and persuaded him to attend church school. This was preferable to doing household chores from which his devout parents excused him. By offering other inducements, the priest managed to teach the boy the four Gospels. In fact, he won a special prize for learning all four by heart and reciting them nonstop in church.

Now 60 years later, he still likes to recite Scriptures, but in a context that would horrify the old priest. For the prize pupil, who memorized so much of the Bible, is Nikita Khrushchev, the former Communist czar."[94]

This story shows that the "why" behind the memorization of Scriptures is as important as the "what." That same Nikita Khrushchev who nimbly mouthed God's Word as a child, later declared God to be nonexistent—because his cosmonauts had not seen Him when they went into space. Khrushchev memorized the Scriptures for the candy, the rewards, and the bribes, rather than for the meaning it had for his life. Artificial motivation will produce artificial results.

Let us not simply commit to the memorization of the Word of God, but let it become part and parcel of our lives. Let us allow the Scriptures to nourish and feed our souls. Jeremiah would say "Thy words were found…and thy word was unto me the joy and rejoicing of my heart…" (Jer. 15:16). And David sang about how he enjoyed His words, declaring them to be "…sweeter also than honey and the honeycomb" (Ps. 19:10).

Jesus also said the Scriptures sustain our spiritual lives as bread nourishes our physical bodies. Matthew records His words, "Man shall not live by bread alone, but by every word that proceeds from the mouth of God" (Matt. 4:4, NKJV).

Kill the Church or Care for It?

Most, if not all of us, are members of the church. And, as members, we are either a support or a burden, an asset or a liability, to the church's forward progress. Whether we are aware of it or not, our actions either propel the church forward or drag it backwards. Christ loves His church, and we all need to show our love and caring for it by supporting His church.

> *Christ loves His church, and we all need to show our love and caring for it by supporting His church.*

The following poem, written by an unknown author, lists things that members do which ruin and ultimately damage or destroy the church.

If You Want to Kill the Church

Never go to your church or to meetings held there.
If you do go, be late; it's no one's affair.
If the weather is bad, either too hot or snowing,
Just stay home and rest, for there'll be others going.

But should you attend, be sure and remember
To find fault with the work, each official and member.
Be sure to hold back on your offerings and tithes,
The bills will be paid by the rest of the guys.

And never take office if offered the post,
But eagerly criticize work of the host.
If not on a committee you're placed, be sore!
If you find that you are, don't attend any more.

When asked your opinion on this thing or that,
Have nothing to say, just turn 'em down flat.
Then after the meeting, shine out like the sun
By telling the folks how it should have been done.

Don't do any more than you possibly can,
Leave the work for some other woman or man.
And when you see faithful ones work themselves sick,
Then stand up and holler, "It's run by a clique!"[95]

    The church is Christ's body, and He is also the Savior of it (Eph. 5:23). He loves His body, and we need to love it too, as we ourselves are part of it (1 Cor. 12:27). May we all show our love by caring and supporting it so "that he might present it to himself a glorious church, not having spot, or wrinkle, or any such thing; but that it should be holy and without blemish" (Eph. 5:27).

The Beggar Who Was King

"Long ago, there ruled in Persia a wise and good king. He loved his people. He wanted to know how they lived. He wanted to know about their hardships. Often he dressed in the clothes of a working man or a beggar, and went to the homes of the poor. No one whom he visited thought that he was their ruler. One time he visited a very poor man who lived in a cellar. He ate the coarse food the poor man ate. He spoke cheerful, kind words to him. Then he left.

Later he visited the poor man again and disclosed his identity by saying,

'I am your king!'

The king thought the man would surely ask for some gift or favor, but he didn't. Instead he said, 'You left your palace and your glory to visit me in this dark, dreary place. You ate the coarse food I ate. You brought gladness to my heart! To others you have given your rich gifts. To me you have given yourself!'"[96]

The King of glory, the Lord Jesus Christ, gave Himself to you and me. The Bible calls Him, "the unspeakable gift!" (2 Cor. 9:15). John 3:16 says, "For God so loved the world, that he gave his only begotten Son, that whosoever believeth in him should not perish, but have everlasting life."

God gave His Son and the Son gave His life so that we can have forgiveness of sins, inherit heaven, and have eternal life. What do we give in return?

This year, let us give God something. Let us give Him our hearts.

Loving Ourselves

I was talking with a new acquaintance, and we were sharing things of common interest to us. He talked about a book he was currently reading in which the author talks about narcissism or the love of self in its most positive light.

The author's approach was to look at self-love on a scale of 1–10, in which both extremes should be avoided. On one extreme, a narcissistic person (who scores in the range of 8–10 on the scale) may love himself so much that he makes himself the center of the universe and tries to order everything to his own advantage and pleasure. The other extreme is the person (who scores in the range of 1–3 on the scale) who deprives himself of every pleasure and benefit and may even physically mortify himself in order to find meaning and significance in life.

We need to go the way of the golden mean (the "average")—and be the person in the range of 4–7 on the scale who loves himself just the right amount. He doesn't love himself too much, in the sense that he esteems himself more highly than others; nor does he hate himself to the point where he sees himself only as trash.

With this in mind, we can better understand the words of Jesus when He gave us the command to love our neighbor as we love ourselves (Matt. 22:39). Because there is no way we can really love our neighbor if we have not truly loved ourselves in the first place. And when we read the instruction about hating father or mother, wife or children, brothers and sisters, or our own lives (Luke 14:26), the text simply means not to "hate" but to "love less."—to love ourselves less than other people. This is where the median range of 4–7 on the scale of love of self comes in instead of the 8–10 range on the scale of extreme self-love.

We must love ourselves appropriately. E.G. White says that the value of a soul can only be measured by the price that was paid by Christ on the cross of Calvary.[97] We are so precious that Christ paid with His blood to set us free. And when we think of what the apostle Paul said that our bodies are the temple of the Holy Spirit and a dwelling place of God (1 Cor. 3:16), we cannot help but love ourselves truly and even reverence our bodies because of the value heaven has placed on them.

Making the Devil Flee

At one of our midweek prayer meetings, we talked about the table of showbread, a piece of furniture in the Holy Place in the earthly sanctuary. The bread points to Jesus who Himself said, "I am the bread of life. He who comes to Me shall never hunger, and he who believes in Me shall never thirst" (John 6:35, NKJV). We need to ask God to give us an appetite for His Word!

As the bread was kept ever before the presence of the Lord, so we must eat every day of this bread for our spiritual nourishment and strength. The disciples didn't understand when Jesus said they needed to eat His flesh and drink His blood. Of course, He was referring to His words as He explains in John 6:63: "It is the Spirit who gives life; the flesh profits nothing. The words that I speak to you are spirit, and they are life" (NKJV).

> *We need to ask God to give us an appetite for His Word!*

We need to ask God to give us an appetite for His Word. For when we regularly partake of this spiritual bread, our character develops and forms according to His likeness. And what is more, this helps us in our fight against the devil.

Here is what happens to the enemy when we get serious with our Bible study.

"When you carry a Bible…the devil gets a headache.

When you open it… he collapses.

When he sees you reading it… he faints.

When he sees you living it…he flees."[98]

Let us spend time with the Word. Let us carry one all the time, open, and read it every day, living out its principles in our lives; and let the enemy of our souls get a headache, collapse, faint, and then finally flee from us.

Tribute to Mothers

This weekend belongs to mothers. It is a special opportunity for fathers and children to show how much they love and appreciate mothers. Some will show their love and affection with flowers or by dining at some fancy restaurant. Others will give cards and chocolate candies. Still others may express their affection and gratitude by doing the chores in the home and giving mothers time off from these household chores that they voluntarily take upon themselves.

Come to think about it, wouldn't it be nice if we made every day of the year a Mother's Day? After all, Mother's Day is a special day to remind us how valuable mothers are, so that we don't forget to show them how much we value them and cherish their love.

The following is a poem written by a grateful child. It expresses the deepest thoughts and sentiments of children who are appreciative of their moms. Its title is "My Mother."

"Your love, I know—I've seen your tears;
You've given to me my life.
You've walked through hours and days and years
Of heartache, toil, and strife.

To see that I could have the best
That you could give to me,
You gave up needs and often rest—
You viewed eternity.

To do His will my highest call
And by your special care
I stood and walked and did not fall,
You held me up in prayer.

Though strands of gray may brush your hair,
And miles divide our way,
I know that by your quiet prayer
You've helped me day by day.

You've shown me how to give, to share

To put my own needs last.
You've helped me see and be aware
That life is so soon past.

To spite your love I would not dare,
For there's not another
Who spreads her gentle love and care
Like you—My Loving Mother."[99]

Men and Women the World Needs Today

We have read amazing stories of the great Scottish explorer and missionary doctor to Africa, David Livingstone. He gave his life and was willing to spend and be spent for the good of the natives who were the objects of his love and sacrifice.[100]

In return, he was loved and cherished by the people. In fact, we learn that, when he died and his remains were to be shipped home to Britain and be ultimately interred at Westminster Abbey, London, the African natives and his loyal attendants thought it proper to have his heart buried there under a tree in the village where he had served because they knew his heart belonged to them.

That he suffered a great deal of hardship and privation during the course of his ministry and service was common knowledge. But this meant nothing to him, as his heart was committed to the good of the people who were the objects of his love.

One time, "a missionary society wrote to him and asked, 'Have you found a good road to where you are? If so, we want to know how to send other men to join you.'

Livingstone wrote back, 'If you have men who will come only if they know there is a good road, I don't want them. I want men who will come if there is no road at all'."[101]

The pioneering and missionary spirit doesn't look for paved roads or smooth sailing. It only asks if there are people desperately waiting to be helped, and then it finds a way to get there and bring the needed love and care.

Do you have that spirit? Are you that one?

The Battle is the Lord's

I find the story recorded in 2 Chronicles, chapter 20, to be very encouraging. The armies of Moab, Ammon, and Mount Seir (descendants of Lot and Esau) had come to fight against God's people. When Jehoshaphat, king of Judah, was told about it, he panicked because he knew there was no way he could fight against such a great multitude. A physical battle between them and the armies of Israel would bring certain defeat.

The king, however, did something else that he should have done in the first place—and it provides a lesson that all of us should learn from. He called all the inhabitants of Jerusalem and Judah to the temple to pray, to fast, to sing, and to praise the Lord—seeking His face and asking for deliverance from their enemies. God's answer, through His messenger, was so encouraging. The prophet told King Jehoshaphat not to panic or worry because the battle was not his but the Lord's. he was instructed not to fight because the Lord would do the fighting for them. And then he was told to position himself and to "...stand ye still, and see the salvation of the Lord with you..." (2 Chron. 20:17).

> *Many times we feel overwhelmed by the challenges and problems that come into our lives. We might panic as King Jehoshaphat did, especially in the face of potentially certain defeat by our enemies.*

Sure enough, when the people of Israel marched to face the enemy the next day, they saw the Lord already doing His job. The people of Ammon and Moab were smiting and killing the people of Mt. Seir and, when they were done, they started fighting and killing one another. After the carnage and all that remained were dead bodies, King Jehoshaphat and his people simply went to gather the spoils and treasures from their dead enemies. It took them three days to do this and, when they were done, they went back to Jerusalem with a large amount of the spoils of war, singing and praising God for what He had done for them.

Many times we feel overwhelmed by the challenges and problems that come into our lives. We might panic as King Jehoshaphat did, especially in the face of potentially certain defeat by our enemies. But instead, let's engage God in prayer, singing and praising His most powerful name. Let us remind Him of the wonderful things He has done in the past for us and for His people and then trust that He still has the power and the might to do it again for us. Then let us receive His gracious response: "You will not need to fight in this battle. Position yourselves, stand still and see the salvation of the Lord!" (2 Chron. 17, NKJV).

God Never Makes Mistakes

A friend shared with me a story that illustrates a biblical principle about an attribute of God, and I want to share that story with you.[102]

Long, long ago, there lived a king whose most faithful and trusted servant would say to him in the face of adverse and even tragic circumstances that God is good, He is perfect in His ways, and He never makes mistakes.

One day, the king went hunting with his servant, and he was attacked by a wild animal. His servant came to the rescue and was able to drive the beast away, but not before the king was badly bruised and one of his fingers was bitten off. The king complained that, if God was so good, why would He allow him to be attacked by such a ferocious beast and have his finger bitten off. His servant could only say that it may be difficult to understand but that shouldn't change the fact that God is good and perfect in His ways and that He never makes mistakes.

The king was furious and, in his rage, he had his servant imprisoned for not coming to his aid early enough and then further insulting him with his remarks.

On another day, the king was on one of his hunting trips again, when he came upon a group of savages and was captured by them. This group engaged in human sacrifices and so, when the time came, the king was led to the altar where he was to be sacrificed. But upon closer scrutiny, the savages found out that the king had a missing finger. This stopped the whole procedure because, according to their traditions, they could not sacrifice an imperfect offering to their god. The king was therefore subsequently released.

When the king got back to his kingdom, the news spread to his subjects; his servant who had been jailed reminded the king that God indeed is wise and never makes mistakes. God had allowed the beast to bite his finger off so that he could be spared the tragedy of becoming a human sacrifice at the hands of his captors.

The king countered by saying that if God indeed was wise and never makes mistakes, then why did He allow the servant to be put in jail? The servant answered, "If God didn't allow me to be put in jail, I would have gone hunting with you. And when the savages found they could not sacrifice you, due to your missing finger, they would have taken me to be sacrificed in your place."

Charles Spurgeon penned the following words.

"God is too good to be unkind,
And He is too wise to be mistaken.
And when we cannot trace His hand,
We must trust His heart."[103]

The preceding materials are expressing, in a variety of ways, the words of the apostle Paul when he said, "And we know that all things work together for good to them that love God, to them who are the called according to his purpose" (Rom. 8:28).

The Agony of Defeat

I like watching the Olympic Games (or any sporting event for that matter) because of the spectacular performances that athletes produce in these world-class events. Here one can see human potential pushed to its very limit, following years of disciplined practice and preparation. And I love seeing and hearing the sights and sounds of ecstasy as these victorious ones celebrate after completing extraordinary routines or when they come up to the podium to receive medals, as their countries' flags are raised to the sound of their national anthems.

But behind the scenes, there are scores of others, equally determined and hard-working athletes, who are quietly licking their wounds and struggling with the agony of defeat. If someone didn't make it into the top three finishers, then that person is a loser, and that's a tough pill to swallow. Especially if someone finished fourth. It is often mentioned that there is nothing worse than a fourth-place finish. because, many times, the difference between standing on the podium to receive a medal versus just being with the spectators may simply have been the difference of a few milliseconds.

This is when the hard part happens. The athlete who didn't make it starts criticizing himself harshly and experiences guilt feelings, blaming himself for the loss, for letting his team down and for disappointing millions of his countrymen who pinned their hopes on him being awarded an Olympic medal. This is not to mention the loss of financial worth from future endorsements and other support networks that usually comes to those who are decorated Olympians.

In the world of kinesiology and sports psychology, researchers recommend a way to effectively deal with this situation. The word is *self-compassion*. It is different from self-confidence and self-esteem, in which individuals are encouraged to have feelings of the ability to succeed or encouraged to focus on their self-worth. Self-compassion is simply treating themselves with kindness and compassion and avoiding any harsh or negative self-criticism. Practitioners suggest that these athletes write letters to themselves expressing understanding, kindness, and concern.

Paul was well aware of the ecstasies of success and the agonies of defeat in the Olympic Games of his day. And he said that those who compete do it to obtain a perishable crown. In the spiritual race that we chose to run, however, we will struggle. Those who run in the Games do it for a temporary crown, we do it to earn an immortal one; and while only three athletes can stand on the medal podium, all of us can win and stand on the medal podium in heaven, if we continue to hold onto Jesus Christ our Lord and Savior and remain faithful to Him to the very end (1 Cor. 9:24–25).

Carelessness in Little Things

In July 1911, a stuntman named Bobby Leach went over Niagara Falls in a specially designed steel drum and lived to tell about it.[104] He did suffer minor injuries but survived because he recognized the tremendous dangers involved in the feat and did everything he could to protect himself.

Years after that incident, while skipping down the street in New Zealand, Bobby Leach slipped on an orange peel. He fell, badly fracturing his leg. He was taken to a hospital but later died of complications from that fall. The irony of this case is that Bobby Leach suffered greater injury walking down a smooth, paved city street than what he sustained going over the rough and turbulent waters of Niagara Falls. The difference could be found in his being alert to the situation and getting prepared for it. He spent precious time and effort strategizing on what he needed to do to come out of a dangerous situation alive and safe, but he was not prepared for danger and was careless in what he assumed to be a safe situation on a city street.

> *Our safety in every situation, however, can be found only in Jesus.*

In our spiritual lives, this is also true. We may be feeling safe, but we can't let down our guard because our "adversary the devil, as a roaring lion, walketh about, seeking whom he may devour" (1 Peter 5:8). And even when we feel confident that we have everything covered and there's no way we can fall, the apostle Paul warns us, "Therefore let him who thinks he stands take heed lest he fall" (1 Cor. 10:12, NKJV).

Our safety in every situation, however, can be found only in Jesus. In life's greatest crises or in the boring routine of our daily grind, the only safe thing to do is to be "looking unto Jesus, the author and finisher of our faith, who for the joy that was set before Him, endured the cross, despising the shame and has sat down at the right hand of the throne of God" (Heb. 12:2, NKJV).

"Greater is He That Is in You"

The apostle John was the longest living apostle among those who were personally associated with Jesus. As such, he was the one privileged to pastor and give guidance and direction to the Christian church of the first century. No wonder that he, with Peter and his brother James, was among those who had been blessed with so many special privileges that were not given to the other nine disciples—because of the need for these experiences and special manifestations for the particular work they were going to do in the future.

John had to contend with the Gnostics, Judaizers, and other false teachers of his day who were avowed enemies of the church. In his first epistle written to the church, he talks about the spirit of the antichrist and the antichrist himself who was already in the world to wreak havoc in the church and with the believers. John warns the believers that while there are manifestations of the true spirit, there were a lot more of the evil kind that were in the world who were out to deceive them with cunning delusions and false teachings. Thus the necessity to "believe not every spirit, but try the spirits whether they are of God…" (1 John 4:1).

The apostle exhorts the Christian believers that they need to stay in the truth and keep faith in Jesus, the Son of God, who came to be manifest in the flesh. And whatever power, strength, or wisdom these spirits may have, they can always be safe in the shelter of the Almighty. In fact he declares, "…greater is he that is in you, than he that is in the world" (1 John 4:4).

To John, the Christian faith is simply trusting in the power of God. The world is full of evil. It is cursed because of the results of the work of the evil one. But we need not fear, nor should we be afraid. In whatever size or shape the challenges or problems may come to us, God is bigger than any of them. Let us remember John's reassuring words, "Greater is He that is in you than he that is in the world."

The Holy Spirit abides in us. That is enough. With Him, we can take care of any problem the devil may throw at us. Let us take John at his word. The Holy Spirit in us is greater than anything there is in this world that may be against us!

Hope in the Land of Captivity

Due to their disobedience and negligence of God's commandments, the people of Israel were allowed by God to be taken into captivity in the land of Babylon. This seemed unjust and harsh, especially considering that the Chaldeans (Babylonians) didn't fear God and were known for their cruelty and savagery. How could God punish the people of Israel using as an instrument a nation that was even more wicked and vile than they were?

Their captors egged them on to sing the songs of Zion while they were in this foreign land. But how could they even do that when they knew Zion was totally desolate and forsaken, and, here they were, living as captives in a foreign land? And so they hung their harps on the willows by the rivers of Babylon as they wept and lamented their seeming hopeless situation.

But God instructed them through His prophets to remain in captivity and live their normal lives. They were to build houses, have their sons and daughters, marry, be given in marriage, plant vineyards, and eat the fruit of them.

The amazing thing about this experience was that, even though they were in the land of captivity, God continued to be with them. No, He had not given up on them. They were going to be there for a time, but in God's own good time, He would visit them and bring them back to their own land. In fact, I find in this instance one of the most reassuring and hopeful promises in the Scriptures—when God says through His prophet Jeremiah, "For I know the plans I have for you, declares the LORD, plans to prosper you and not to harm you, plans to give you hope and a future" (Jer. 29:11, NIV).

That's what is so amazing about God. Due to our disobedience and rebelliousness towards His will, He may allow us to go into the land of captivity—of ill health, financial setbacks, or failed relationships. He is not going to perform a miracle to save us from suffering the consequences of our wrong decisions and stubborn will, but He does not leave us there. He does not give us up. We are so precious to Him, and He assures us of His continued care, as He insists that whoever touches us "touches the apple of His eye" (Zech. 2:8).

So let us not get discouraged, however difficult our situation may be—whether going through a storm or walking through a valley. Let us continue to trust in Him because, indeed, He knows the plans He has for us, and these are plans that are not meant to harm us but to prosper us—to give us hope and a future. There is hope even in the land of our captivity. In God's own time, He will visit us again and bring us back to His own eternal land.

Do We See the Little Bandaged Fingers?

Dwight Morrow, one-time United States senator, ambassador to Mexico, and the father of Anne Morrow Lindbergh (an American writer and decorated aviator in her own right), "once held a dinner party to which Calvin Coolidge had been invited.

After Coolidge left, Morrow told the remaining guests that Coolidge would make a good president. The others disagreed. They felt Coolidge was too quiet, that he lacked color and personality.

'No one would like him', they said.

Anne, then age six, spoke up: 'I like him,' she said. Then she displayed a finger with a small bandage around it. "He was the only one at the party who asked about my sore finger.'

'And that's why he would make a good president,' added Morrow."[105]

As we journey through life, we will see that all around us are people who are hurting and in need of some care and attention. Some may have a little bandaged finger. Others may be suffering from some kind of discomfort or another. And all they may need is a word from us that we have seen their hurt and understand their pain.

Do we even take time for these seemingly inconsequential things? When Jesus said, "The poor you will always have with you..." (Matt.26:11), He meant that it is God's plan for us to be exposed to the needs of the poor and the suffering. Because, when that happens, our finer sensibilities are aroused, and a compassionate, tender, and caring spirit can then flow spontaneously from our otherwise calloused hearts.

> *As we journey through life, we will see that all around us are people who are hurting and in need of some care and attention.*

We may not be running for the presidency of the United States. But a caring and compassionate heart is what we must have if we are to develop a character like that of Christ and be fit to be citizens of His Kingdom. We can never be like God until our hearts are broken by the things that break the heart of God.

One Dark Night in Las Vegas

What happened in Las Vegas, Nevada, in 2017 is still a subject of conversation across the country—in small groups, on radio talk shows, on television programs, and on social media. A person, who was supposed to be enjoying the good life established a perch in his suite on the thirty-second floor of Mandalay Bay Resort and, for 11 minutes, rained bullets on thousands of defenseless people who were in the city that weekend to attend a country music concert. Fifty-eight people died (including the gunman) and over 500 people were injured, some seriously, and others were permanently handicapped and disabled for life.[106]

At that point in time, this was the deadliest mass shooting in United States history.

Whatever this person's motives were, what happened simply highlights certain facts about the world we are living in.

1. A man can plunge into the depths of evil no matter how great his fortune or how well-positioned in society he may be.

2. A place of fun and laughter can suddenly turn into a place of carnage and mourning.

3. Just one man's evil mind and sinister actions can lead to so much sorrow and pain.

4. There is no way one can guarantee peace, safety, or security in this world.

5. Guns and ammunition that may originally have been intended to protect and defend can easily fall into wrong hands and be used to destroy innocent lives and unsuspecting people.

6. Times of crisis bring out the best in people, as shown by the heroic acts of so many who shielded others from the bullets with their own bodies and who attended to the needs of the fallen and the wounded, by taking them to a place of safety where they could get help—at the risk of their own lives.

7. A world of darkness is just the place where God's people must stand up and let their lights shine.

The only choice we have is to let our lights shine brighter than those in the world (Matt. 5:16) and make our message ring louder and clearer that there is a better world to come, where peace, love, and joy eternally dwell. We need to double our efforts in reaching out to this dark and perishing world. When this is done, under the blessing and power of the Holy Spirit, Jesus will establish His kingdom that will last forever, and then His will may done on earth as it is in heaven.

A Letter to Dads

We appreciate what fathers do for us, but we do not always take the time to let them know about it. And just like we sometimes say, "Better late than never," we can always write a letter detailing to them how much we value the time they have spent with us and the sacrifices they have made for us—and will continue to make to make our lives pleasant, comfortable, and fulfilling.

This poem will make the fathers in our lives happy, and we will be glad we were able to express what has been in our hearts and minds all along and what they have meant to our lives.

"Dear Dad
There are so many things I'd like
To tell you face to face;
I either lack the words or fail
To find the time and place.
But in this special letter, Dad,
You'll find, at least in part,
The feeling that the passing years
Have left within my heart.
The memory of childhood days
And all that you have done,
To make our home a happy place
And growing up such fun!
I still recall the walks we took,
The games we often played;
Those confidential talks we had
While resting in the shade.
This letter comes to thank you, Dad,
For needed words of praise;
The counsel and the guidance, too,
That shaped my grown-up days.
No words of mine can tell you, Dad,
The things I really feel;
But you must know my love for you

Is lasting, warm, and real.
You made my world a better place,
And through the coming years;
I'll keep these memories of you
As cherished souvenirs. ..."[107]

Happy Father's Day to all the fathers out there. Our lives are greatly blessed because of you. May you live long, healthy, and happy lives!

A Time for Celebration?

Author Leo Buscaglia tells this story about his mother and their "misery dinner." It was the night after his father came home and said it looked as if he would have to go into bankruptcy because his partner had absconded with their firm's funds. His mother went out and sold some jewelry to buy food for a sumptuous feast. Other members of the family scolded her for it. But she told them that "the time for joy is now, when we need it most, not next week." Her courageous act rallied the family,[108] and they went on to face the future with courage and hope.

Things happen. While we are on this side of heaven, we experience financial setbacks, failing health, and broken relationships. What we do when we lose a substantial investment or when we receive a grim prognosis about our health or the health of that of a loved one determines the quality of life we will have for the remainder of our days.

> *When we go through tough times and walk through the valley, we may not feel like lighting fireworks, but we still can celebrate, can't we?*

No, we don't go and sulk in a corner. We don't close the blinds and pull the shutters down, isolating ourselves from the rest of the world. Let's bring out the china and enjoy a rich repast. Let's give ourselves a taste once more of that favorite ice cream flavor we have missed for so long. Let's get out to the meadows and enjoy the cool breeze and the warm sunshine. Let's thank God that, in spite of the setbacks we have, we still have moments left to savor of what remains of life and then praise His awesome name.

And who knows if this positive attitude and extraordinary optimism we have found can turn things around and reverse whatever bad fix we have found ourselves in.

Remember David? He mourned, fasted, and lay all night upon the earth while his baby struggled at the point of death. And yet, when the baby died, he washed his face and came to the table to eat. He said, "While the child was yet alive, I fasted and wept: for I said, Who can tell whether GOD will be gracious to me, that the child may live? But now he is dead, wherefore should I fast? can I bring him back again? I shall go to him, but he shall not return to me" (2 Sam. 12:22–23).

When we go through tough times and walk through the valley, we may not feel like lighting fireworks, but we still can celebrate, can't we?

A Tragedy or a Blessing?

"Years ago in Scotland, the Clark family had a dream. The husband and his wife worked and saved, making plans for their 9 children and themselves to travel to the United States. After many years, they had enough money and passports to make reservations for the family to sail on a new liner to the United States.

The family was filled with anticipation and excitement about their new life. But 7 days before their departure, the youngest son was bitten by a dog. The doctor sewed up the boy but hung a yellow sheet on the Clarks' front door, signaling a household quarantine for 14 days because of the possibility of rabies.

> *For all we know, the bitter experiences in life are God's way of preserving us and getting us ready for something more glorious than what we have ever imagined.*

The family's dreams were dashed. They couldn't make the trip to America as planned. The father, filled with disappointment and anger, stomped to the dock to watch the ship leave without the Clark family. He shed tears of disappointment and cursed both his son and God for their misfortune.

Five days later, the tragic news spread throughout Scotland—the mighty *Titanic* had sunk. The unsinkable ship had taken hundreds of lives. The Clark family was to have been on that ship, but because the son had been bitten by a dog, they were left behind in Scotland.

When the father heard the news, he ran home, hugged his son, and thanked him for saving the family. He thanked God for saving their lives and turning what he knew was a tragedy into a blessing."[109]

At times, we lament our misfortune when things happen or don't happen according to our plans and desires. But we need to remember that life is in constant motion, and we must hold off giving our verdict until the real-life drama has fully unfolded. For all we know, the bitter experiences in life are God's way of preserving us and getting us ready for something more glorious than what we have ever imagined. We see them as tragedies, but God intends them for us to be blessings. The Scriptures say, "And we know that all things work together for good to them that love God, to them who are the called according to his purpose" (Rom. 8:28).

Let Them Hear It Now

British historian and philosopher Thomas Carlyle had a very devoted wife who sacrificed much for his sake.

After her death, Carlyle, while reading her diary, realized the truth. She had longed to spend more time with him while she was dying. A friend found him at her grave, suffering intense remorse and exclaiming, "If I had only known!"[110]

> *So while our loved ones are still able to feel, hear, and experience our love and affection for them, let us show them.*

Carlyle's experience brings to mind the song "If Tomorrow Never Comes,"[111] which was written by Ronan Keating and popularized by country singer Garth Brooks. The song tells about how the songwriter lost loved ones in his life who never knew how much he loved them, and how he was living with the regret that his true feelings for them had never been revealed. He then promised himself to say each day how much she (his wife) means to him, and avoid the circumstance in which there's no second chance to tell her how he feels

So while our loved ones are still able to feel, hear, and experience our love and affection for them, let us show them. Thereby, we avoid any circumstance of regret that we never had a second chance to tell them how we felt. Now is the time to tell and show them our love. There may never be a second chance. Even the Scriptures say, "Boast not thyself of to morrow; for thou knowest not what a day may bring forth" (Prov. 27:1).

Built on a Rock

"Gregory Elder tells of growing up on the Atlantic Coast, where he spent long hours working on intricate sandcastles. One year, for several days in a row, he was confronted by bullies who smashed his creations. Finally he tried an experiment: He placed cinder blocks, rocks, and chunks of concrete in the base of his castles. Then he built the sand kingdoms on top of the rocks. When the local toughs appeared (and he disappeared), their bare feet suddenly met their match."[112]

Many people see the church in great peril from a variety of dangers in these last days: worldliness, political meddling, papal and religious interventions, heresies, or gross sinfulness. They forget that the church is built upon a Rock, ...and the gates of hell itself shall not prevail against it" (Matt. 16:18).

When Simon Peter said, "Thou art the Christ, the Son of the living God (Matt.16:16), Jesus assured Peter and His disciples, and He assures all of us as well, by telling Simon Peter, "Blessed art thou, Simon Barjona: for flesh and blood hath not revealed it unto thee, but my Father which is in heaven. And I say also unto thee, That thou art Peter, and upon this rock I will build my church; and the gates of hell shall not prevail against it' (Matt. 16:17—18).

So let's not worry or be anxious about the church. It may even seem as if it is about to fall, but it will not fall. It is God's church, and He will take care of it and protect it as the apple of His eye.

Contrary to what many think, Peter was not the rock that Jesus built His church on. Jesus said the gates of hell shall not prevail against the church's foundation, whereas Peter...—well, he crumbled a short time later at the crowing of the cock! The Rock on which Jesus built the church was Himself. It was by contrast that Jesus spoke to Peter and actually said, "Peter, you are a smooth, rolling stone…and upon this Rock (alluding to Himself) I will build My church."

There is no other Rock that the Scriptures talk about other than the Rock Christ Jesus (Ps. 18:2, 31, 46; 1 Cor. 10:4 and many more verses). Even Peter concedes and acknowledge that Jesus Himself is the Rock (1 Peter 2:8).

So let's not worry or be anxious about the church. It may even seem as if it is about to fall, but it will not fall. It is God's church, and He will take care of it and protect it as the apple of His eye.

Backward, Christian Soldiers!

Most of us are familiar with that favorite hymn in our Seventh-day Adventist hymnal, "Onward, Christian Soldiers!"[113] We have sang this at our Pathfinder and Adventurer Investiture programs and youth rallies, and we have used it as a battle cry for our evangelism campaigns. And this is good, because it is a rallying song, and it is meant to rouse everyone to stand up and join Christ's army and march along to the fray.

But do we just talk and sing about going to war? Do we actually pick up our spiritual swords and shields and engage the enemy to fight? Does our daily life belie all of our shoutings and proclamations of war?

Someone did a rewrite of the above-mentioned hymn to reflect what he thinks is actually happening in the spiritual lives of Christians these days. As you read the hymn in its revised form, ask yourself, "Does this tell the real story of the church today?" And, more importantly, "Does this give a true reflection of my participation in the great controversy between the forces of good and evil?

"Backward Christian Soldiers
Backward Christian soldiers, Fleeing from the fight,
With the cross of Jesus, Nearly out of sight.
Christ our rightful master, Stands against the foe;
Onward into battle, we seem afraid to go.
Backward Christian soldiers, Fleeing from the fight,
With the cross of Jesus, Nearly out of sight.

Like a might tortoise, Moves the church of God.
Brothers we are treading, Where we've often trod.
We are much divided, Many bodies we,
Having different doctrines, but not much charity.

Crowns and thrones may perish, Kingdoms rise and wane,
But the cross of Jesus, Hidden does remain.
Gates of hell should never 'gainst the Church prevail,
We have Christ's own promise, But we think it might fail.

Sit here then ye people, Join our sleeping throng.
Blend with ours, your voices in a feeble song.

Blessings, ease and comfort, Ask from Christ the King,
But with our modern thinking, We won't do a thing.
Backward Christian soldiers, Fleeing from the fight,
With the cross of Jesus, Nearly out of sight."[114]

If the anonymous writer who revised this hymn is correct, it's not too late to change. We can do something about it. And more importantly, the Holy Spirit can help us do something about it, to show what God would be pleased to see in His church.

Paul says, "Finally, my brethren, be strong in the Lord, and in the power of His might. Put on the whole armour of God, that ye may be able to stand against the wiles of the devil.

For we wrestle not against flesh and blood, but against principalities, against powers, against the rulers of the darkness of this world, against spiritual wickedness in high places. Wherefore take unto you the whole armour of God, that ye may be able to withstand in the evil day, and having done all, to stand.

Stand therefore, having your loins girt about with truth, and having on the breastplate of righteousness; And your feet shod with the preparation of the gospel of peace; Above all, taking the shield of faith, wherewith ye shall be able to quench all the fiery darts of the wicked. And take the helmet of salvation, and the sword of the Spirit, which is the word of God..." (Eph. 6:10-17).

The Da Vinci Code

Dan Brown's novel, *The Da Vinci Code*, generated a great deal of interest and was made into a major motion picture.

The story line of this novel/motion picture attacks the very heart of the gospel and attempts to destroy the very nature and character of the Lord Jesus Christ as the Son of God. It portrays Jesus Christ as marrying Mary Magdalene and having children with her; it claims that His physical bloodline continues in France to this day. It also claims that this secret was kept by a religious order for hundreds of years, and that it was also encoded in one of the great artist Leonardo da Vinci's paintings.[115]

We know that this is all a figment of the imagination. It is nothing but a lie inspired by the Evil One. There is absolutely no truth to it, and yet it has the potential to deceive millions, discrediting the Scriptures as the Word of God and Jesus as God's own Son.

We can do one of two things or, better yet, both. We can pray the prayer of Jesus for the author and the entire cast: "Father, forgive them for they know not what they do." And we can look at this crisis as one more opportunity to strike up a conversation about Jesus and tell people who He really is—in our lives and for all mankind.

Making Sense of the World

A father was busy reading a magazine when his little daughter, Susie, came and asked him to play with her. He didn't want to be bothered, so he took a page out of the magazine, on which was printed a map of the world. Tearing it into small pieces, he gave it to Susie and said, "Go into your room and see if you can put this together."

After a few minutes, Susie returned and handed him the map, correctly fitted together. The father was very surprised and asked how she had finished so quickly.

"Oh," she said, "on the other side of the paper is a picture of Jesus. When I got Jesus in His place, then the world came out all right."[116]

Having Jesus in the right place is not just the secret of putting the pieces of a puzzle together. It is also the secret to having peace in the world and in our lives.

So, do we have Jesus in His rightful place? Is He in our own hearts, and is He the ruler of our lives?

Cell Phones Versus the Bible

We live in an age of technological advancement and innovation. And one of the greatest blessings in the field of communication technology is the cell phone. Because of its availability and practical usefulness, we can reach people anytime, anywhere and, in the same way, people can reach us whenever and wherever we are. In the urban centers of the great cities of the world, in a busy amusement park, or even in the remotest jungles of the Third World, we are able to connect with those we want to get in touch with, either in emergency situations or simply for conversational pleasure.

No doubt, the cell phone is a boon. But have you wondered what things would be like if we treated our Bible in the same way we do our cell phones? The following material gives us something to think about if we used our Bible the same way we use our cell phones.

"I wonder what would happen if we treated our Bible like we treat our cell phone?

What if we carried it around in our purses or pockets?

What if we flipped through it several times a day?

What if we turned back to go get it if we forgot it?

What if we used it to receive messages from the text?

What if we treated it like we couldn't live without it?

What if we gave it to kids as gifts?

What if we used it as we traveled?

What if we used it in case of emergency?

Oh, and one more thing. Unlike our cell phones, we don't have to worry about our Bible being disconnected because Christ already paid the bill. And no dropped calls."[117]

Now my friend…where is that Bible of yours?

The Twenty-Third Psalm

Especially for those of us who were raised in Adventist homes, we are blessed with a rich memory bank of Scripture texts and songs. But the downside of this is the familiarity we have with these verses, so that we tend to take them for granted and fail to look at them with inquisitive minds and eyes of wonder. Just like the so-called "Shepherd Psalm" (Ps. 23:1–6). Have you ever looked at it this way?

"The Lord is my Shepherd—

> That's RELATIONSHIP!

I shall not want—

> That's SUPPLY!

He maketh me to lie down in green pastures—

> That's REST!

He leadeth me beside still waters—

> That's REFRESHMENT!

He restoreth my soul—

> That's HEALING!

He leadeth me in the paths of righteousness—

> That's GUIDANCE!

For His name's sake—

> That's PURPOSE!

Yea, though I walk through the valley of the shadow of death,

> [That's TESTING!]

I will fear no evil—

    That's PROTECTION!

For Thou are with me—

    That's FAITHFULNESS!

Thy rod and thy staff they comfort me—

    That's COMFORT!

Thou preparest a table before me in the presence of mine enemies—

    That's HOPE!

Thou anointest my head with oil—

    That's CONSECRATION!

My cup runneth over—

    That's ABUNDANCE!

Surely goodness and mercy shall follow me all the days of my life—

    That's BLESSING!

And I will dwell in the house of the Lord—

    That's SECURITY!

Forever—

    That's ETERNITY!"[118]

When it comes down to it, what is valuable is not what we have in our lives but Who we have in our lives! So, do you know the Shepherd?

Signs of Spiritual Awakening

The following has been shared with me, and it is good material that gives specific signs of a spiritual life. It would be nice to know whether we have been quickened by the Holy Spirit; and if these marks do not show in our lives, then it is high time to seek to be born again—which is the only way one can enter into the kingdom of God (John 3:3–5). Here are some of the signs of a spiritual life.

"1. An increased tendency to let things happen rather than make them happen.

2. Frequent attacks of smiling.

3. Feelings of being connected with others and nature.

4. Frequent overwhelming episodes of appreciation.

5. A tendency to think and act spontaneously rather than from fears based on past experience.

6. An unmistakable ability to enjoy each moment.

7. A loss of ability to worry.

8. A loss of interest in conflict.

9. A loss of interest in interpreting the actions of others.

10. A loss of interest in judging others.

11. A loss of interest in judging self.

12. Gaining the ability to love without expecting anything in return."[119]

"No Time for God?

I knelt to pray but not for long,
I had too much to do.
I had to hurry and get to work
For bills would soon be due.

So I knelt and said a hurried prayer,
And jumped up off my knees.
My Christian duty was now done,
My soul could rest at ease.

All day long I had no time
To spread a word of cheer.
No time to speak of Christ to friends,
They'd laugh at me I'd fear.

'No time, no time, too much to do,'
That was my constant cry.
No time to give to souls in need.
But at last the time, the time to die.

I went before the Lord, I came,
I stood with downcast eyes.
For in His hands, God held a book,
It was the book of life.

God looked into His book and said,
'Your name I cannot find.
I once was going to write it down
But never found the time.'"[120]

> *What if God gave us an amount of time that was equal to what we give to Him? Would it be something we would be happy about?*

What if God gave us an amount of time that was equal to what we give to Him? Would it be something we would be happy about? Paul says, "For in him we live, and move, and have our being" (Acts 17:28). Which means that there is no way we can have time apart from God's providence. I pray we give Him back the precious time that He so graciously gives us, and we make Him first place in everything in our lives.

Aging Gracefully

I want to share with you some excellent material that was sent to me recently. I entitled it, "Aging Gracefully," because it outlines certain principles of living that we can all go by that will help us to be happy and contented, even through our later years. Here they are:

1. "Never say 'I am aged'. There are three ages: chronological, biological, and psychological. The first is calculated based on our date of birth; the second is determined by the health conditions; the third is how old we feel we are. While we don't have control over the first, we can take care of our health with good diet, exercise, and a cheerful attitude. A positive attitude and optimistic thinking can reverse the third age."[121]

2. "Health is wealth. If you really love your kids and kin, taking care of yourself and your health should be your priority. Thus, you will not be a burden to them. Have an annual health check-up and take the prescribed medicines regularly. Do take health insurance coverage.

3. Money is important. Money is essential for meeting the basic necessities of life, keeping good health and earning family respect and security. Don't spend beyond your means even for your children. You have lived for them all through [your life], and it is time you enjoyed a harmonious life with your spouse. If your children are grateful and they take care of you, you are blessed. But never take it for granted.

4. Relaxation and recreation. The most relaxing and recreating forces are a healthy religious attitude, good sleep, music and laughter. Have faith in God, learn to sleep well, love good music and see the funny side of life.

5. Time is precious. It is almost like holding a horse's reins. When they are in your hands, you can control them. Imagine that every day you are born again. Yesterday is a cancelled check.

Tomorrow is a promissory note. Today is ready cash—use it profitably. Live this moment.

6. Change is the only permanent thing. We should accept change—it is inevitable. The only way to make sense out of change is to join the dance. Change has brought about many pleasant things. We should be happy that our children are blessed.

7. Enlightened selfishness. All of us are basically selfish. Whatever we do, we expect something in return. We should definitely be grateful to those who stood by us. But our focus should be on the internal satisfaction and happiness we derive by doing good to others, without expecting anything in return.

8. Forgive and forget. Don't be bothered too much about others' mistakes. We are not spiritual enough to show our other cheek when we are slapped on one. But for the sake of our own health and happiness, let us forgive and forget them. Otherwise, we will be only increasing our blood pressure.

9. Everything has a reason, a purpose. Take life as it comes. Accept yourself as you are and also accept others for what they are. Everybody is unique and right in his own way.

10. Overcome the fear of death. We all know that one day we have to leave this world. Still we are afraid of death. We think that our spouse and children will be unable to withstand our loss. But the truth is no one is going to die for you; they may be depressed for some time. Time heals everything and they will carry on."[122]

Moses, who wrote the Psalm 90, said, "The days of our lives are seventy years and if by reason of strength they are eighty years, yet their boast is only labor and sorrow…" (Ps. 90:10, NKJV).

So he prays, "Teach us to number our days, that we may gain a heart of wisdom" (Ps. 90:12, NKJV).

Even the life we have here on earth is precious. Christ purchased it with His own blood. Use it to honor God and bless your fellow man. Treasure it. Cherish it. Enjoy it. It is God's gift to you.

Twenty-Six Guards

"A missionary on furlough told this true story while visiting his home church in Michigan.

'While serving at a small field hospital in Africa, every two weeks I traveled by bicycle through the jungle to a nearby city for supplies. This was a journey of two days and required camping overnight at the halfway point.'

'On one of these journeys, I arrived in the city where I planned to collect money from a bank, purchase medicine, and supplies, and then begin my two-day journey back to the field hospital.'

'Upon arrival in the city, I observed two men fighting, one of whom had been seriously injured. I treated him for his injuries and at the same time witnessed to him of the Lord Jesus Christ.'

'I then traveled two days, camped overnight, and arrived home without incident.'

'Two weeks later I repeated my journey.'

'Upon arriving in the city, I was approached by the young man I had treated. He told me that he had known I carried money and medicines. He said, 'Some friends and I followed you into the jungle, knowing you would camp overnight. We planned to kill you and take your money and drugs. But just as we were about to move into your camp, we saw that twenty-six armed guards surrounded you.'

'At this, I laughed and said that I was certainly all alone out in that jungle campsite.'

'The young man pressed the point, however, and said, 'No, sir, I was not the only person to see the guards, my five friends also saw them, and we all counted them. It was because of those guards that we were afraid and left you alone.'

At this point in the sermon, one of the men in the congregation jumped to his feet and interrupted the missionary and asked if he could tell him the exact day this happened.

The missionary told the congregation the date, and the man who interrupted told him this story.

'On the night of your incident in Africa, it was morning here and I was preparing to go play golf. I was about to putt when I felt the urge to pray for you. In fact, the urging of the Lord was so strong, I called men in this church to meet with me here in the sanctuary to pray for you. Would all of those men who met with me on that day stand up?'

The men who had met together to pray that day stood up. The missionary wasn't concerned with who they were—he was too busy counting how many men he saw.

There were twenty-six."[123]

This story is an incredible example of the mysterious workings of the Holy Spirit. So when you feel the promptings of the Spirit, go with It and allow yourself to be an instrument in God's hand to accomplish His purpose.

Living to Bless Others

Life is uncertain. Realize that God has put us here on earth to serve Him and to help those who are in need along life's way. "I once read about a university professor who, many years ago, was invited to speak at a military base. A young soldier named Ralph had been sent to meet him at the airport. After introducing himself, they headed for the baggage claim.

As they made their way there, Ralph kept getting sidetracked. He first stopped to help an older woman whose suitcase had fallen open. On another occasion, he lifted two toddlers up to see Santa Claus. Once, he stopped to give directions to people who appeared not to know their way.

> *Life is uncertain. Realize that God has put us here on earth to serve Him and to help those who are in need along life's way.*

Finally, the professor asked, 'Where did you learn to do that?'

'What?' the soldier responded.

'Where did you learn to live like that, taking so much time for people?' the professor explained.

'I guess it was during the war in Vietnam,' Ralph said. He explained that it had been his job to clear the minefields, and he had watched many of his friends get blown up in front of his eyes.

"'I learned to live between the steps,' he said. 'I never knew when one step might be my last, so I learned to get everything I can out of the moment between when I picked up my foot and when I put it down again.'"[124]

We don't have to go on a tour of duty in a war zone to learn that life is so uncertain and to realize that God has put us here on earth to serve Him and help those in need along life's way.

So let our next step lead us to bless those in need of our help and live our lives, following after Him who came not "…to be served, but to serve, and to give His life a ransom for many" (Matt. 20:28, NKJV).

As John Wesley once said,

"Do all the good you can,
By all the means you can,
In all the ways you can,
In all the places you can,
At all the times you can,
To all the people you can,
As long as ever you can."[125]

Some Valuable Quotes

Let me share some quotes that could help open your eyes a bit about church life.

"Don't let your worries get the best of you—remember, Moses started out as a basket case.

Some people are kind, polite, and sweet-spirited—until you try to sit in their pews.

Many folks want to serve God—but only as advisors…

People are funny; they want the front of the bus, the middle of the road and—the back of the church!

Opportunity may knock once—but temptation bangs on your front door forever.

Quit griping about your church; if it was perfect, you couldn't belong.

If the church wants a better pastor—it only needs to pray for the one it has.

God Himself does not propose to judge a man until he is dead—so why should you?

Some minds are like concrete—thoroughly mixed up and permanently set.

Peace starts with—a smile.

I don't know why some people change churches; what difference does it make which one you stay home from?"[126]

"A lot of church members who are singing 'Standing on the Promises' are just sitting on the premises.

Be ye fishers of men. You catch them. He'll clean them.

Don't wait for six strong men to take you to church.

Forbidden fruits create many jams.

God loves everyone, but probably prefers 'fruits of the spirit' over 'religious nuts!'[127]

People Need the Lord

September 11, 2000, marks the anniversary of the worst terrorist attack on America. When we look back to that infamous and dastardly evil act of unconscionable men, our hearts go out to the families of the more than 3,000 lives that were lost in that tragedy.

But evil is not going to triumph over good. The way the City of New York and the rest of America and the world responded is evidence that God has not left this sinful world alone and that He continues to work in the human heart. Hundreds and thousands of police and firemen and regular citizens came to help the wounded and the dying and, in the process, many gave their lives in a supreme act of heroism, courage, and sacrifice.

Today, years later, America continues to engage in this war on terror. And although many parts of the world have been infected by this evil philosophy, America is committed to stand and defend herself against anyone that would threaten her freedom and her way of life.

On the religious front, America's churches suddenly filled with worshipers, immediately following the tragedy. Attendance soared to an all-time high. Churches suddenly were faced with the challenge of meeting the needs of so many fearful and troubled hearts.

If there is something we can learn from all of this, it is the fact that people need the Lord, and it doesn't matter if times are good or bad. We need Him in times of trouble. And in times of peace and prosperity, He is still our hearts' desire. There is a void in the human heart that no one else but God can fill. As St. Augustine prayed, "Thou hast made us for Thyself, O Lord, and our heart is restless until it finds its rest in Thee!"[128]

> *People need the Lord, and it doesn't matter if times are good or bad. We need Him in times of trouble. And in times of peace and prosperity, He is still our hearts' desire.*

Things I Wish I Had Known Before I Was Twenty-One

Every now and then we schedule a youth ministry's Pathfinder Sabbath at our church, and we let our young people lead out in our worship services. We highlight them and their club activities and programs. It is also a time to thank our Pathfinder leaders and staff and the parents of these young people for their support of this youth ministry. These types of services are what contribute to the excellence and effectiveness of our youth program at our church.

It was Lyman Bryson who said, "The error of youth is to believe that intelligence is a substitute for experience, while the error of age is to believe that experience is a substitute for intelligence."[129] To avoid these errors of thinking, we need to realize that we need both intelligence and experience—which means that we all need each other if we are to live meaningful lives.

To everyone—and especially to our youth—the following material could be of great help to you as you mature into adulthood and on into your later years. It was written by an anonymous author but the thoughts are great and it would be good for you to ponder upon-

"Things I Wish I Would Have Known Before I was Twenty-One: That a man's habits are mighty hard to change after he is twenty-one.

That a harvest depends on the seeds sown.
That worthwhile things require time, patience, and hard work.
That you cannot get something for nothing.
The folly of not taking other people's advice.

The value of absolute truthfulness in everything.
That what my mother wanted me to do was right.
That Dad wasn't an old fogey after all.
More of the helpful and inspiring messages of the Bible.
The greatness of the opportunity and joy of serving a fellow human being.
That Jesus Christ want to be my Savior and Friend."[130]

Running .... and Finishing the Race

"At 7 p.m. on October 20, 1968, just a few thousand spectators remained in the Mexico City Olympic Stadium. It was cool and dark. The last of the marathon runners, each exhausted, were being carried off to first-aid stations. More than an hour earlier, Mamo Wolde of Ethiopia—looking as fresh as when he started the race—crossed the finish line, the winner of the 26-mile, 385-yard event.

As the remaining spectators prepared to leave, those sitting near the marathon gates suddenly heard the sound of sirens and police whistles. All eyes turned to the gate. A lone figure wearing number 36 and the colors of Tanzania entered the stadium. His name was John Stephen Akhwari. He was the last man to finish the marathon. He had fallen during the race and injured his knee and ankle. Now, with his leg bloodied and bandaged, he grimaced with each hobbling step around the 400-meter track.

The spectators rose and applauded him. After crossing the finish line, Akhwari slowly walked off the field. Later, a reporter asked Akhwari the question on everyone's mind: 'Why did you continue the race after you were so badly injured?'

He replied, 'My country did not send me 7,000 miles to start the race. They sent me 7,000 miles to finish it.'"[131]

As Christians we are all in a race. Some start strong and fast, but they falter when the way becomes steep or they stumble at the last mile of the way. Only those who continue to the end will win the prize. And all of us are assured of help. Paul says in his letter to the Philippians, "For I am confident of this very thing, that He who began a good work in you will bring it to completion until the day of Jesus Christ" (Phil. 1:6, ESV).

And finally, the writer to the Hebrews says, "...And let us run with perseverance the race marked out for us (Heb. 12:1, NIV); looking unto Jesus the author and finisher of our faith; who for the joy that was set before Him, endured the cross, despising the shame, and is set down at the right hand of the throne of God" (Heb. 12:2).

The Little Things

A few days ago, America and the rest of the freedom-loving world celebrated the anniversary of 9/11. There were vigils, rallies, and church services, honoring the memory of the over 3,000 men and women who perished in the senseless and reprehensible act of violence perpetrated on American soil against innocent civilians. Not to be forgotten are the hundreds of police officers, fire fighters, and other volunteers who came to the rescue of the wounded and the dying and who also did the ultimate act of heroism by paying with their own lives. To this day, offices and buildings still carry banners with the sworn inscription, "We shall never forget."

Without trying to divert attention from the victims of 9/11, there are some lessons we can learn from this tragic event. It seems that there might have been more people who perished on that fateful day, except for the fact that they encountered some petty annoyances and trivial matters that delayed them, preventing them from being there at that particular point in time.

"As you might remember, the head of a company survived 9/11 because his son started kindergarten. Another fellow was alive because it was his turn to bring donuts.

One woman was late because her alarm clock didn't go off in time. One was late because of being stuck on the NJ [New Jersey] Turnpike because of an auto accident. One of them missed his bus. Another spilled food on her clothes and had to take time to change. One couldn't get his car to start. One couldn't get a taxi.

The one that struck me was the man who put on a new pair of shoes that morning. He took the various means to get to work but, before he got there, he developed a blister on his foot. He stopped at a drugstore to buy a Band-Aid.® That is why he is alive today.

Now when I am stuck in traffic, miss an elevator, turn back to answer a ringing telephone…all the little things that annoy me, I think to myself: This is exactly where God wants me to be at this very moment.

Next time your morning seems to be going wrong—the children are slow getting dressed, you can't seem to find the car keys, you hit every traffic light…don't get mad or frustrated. It may just be that God is at work watching over you. May God continue to bless you with all those annoying little things and may you remember their possible purpose."[132]

Every Day Is Special

Have there been times in your life when you bought something nice to wear for a special occasion and something happened and you didn't get the chance to put it on? Or maybe you had a card or a gift for someone for some special event and you were not able to give it to them?

What we need to do to realize is the fact that every day is special. So why not do what you want to do today? Do not wait or save anything for some special occasion. Because, the fact is, every day in your life is special.

So go ahead. Spend more time with your family and friends, even with Christmas and Thanksgiving still months away. Put on some new clothes even when you are just going to the grocery store. Quit saving that perfume for some special occasion. The special occasion is NOW…You continue to use paper plates and Styrofoam cups. How about taking out those long-kept china plates from the cabinet and enjoying them now. Because today is special. And that "special occasion" may never come.

> *Because today is special. And today is all you have.*

Do not delay or keep anything that could bring laughter and joy into your life. Never wait for that special occasion. If anything is worth seeing or listening to or doing, then see and listen to and do it now.

Because today is special. And today is all you have.

You Are Special

Are there times in your life when you feel drained? Your energy level is at rock-bottom and that zest for living is somehow just not there.

It may help to realize that there is more to life than the way you are feeling at times. You may not realize it, but it's all so true. Consider the following when you feel "down."

"1. There are at least two people in this world that you would die for.

2. At least fifteen people in this world love you in some way.

3. The only reason anyone would ever hate you is that they want to be just like you.

4. A smile from you can bring happiness to anyone, even if they don't like you.

5. Every night, SOMEONE thinks about you before they go to sleep.

6. You mean the world to someone.

7. You are special and unique.

8. Someone that you don't even know exists, loves you.

9. When you make the biggest mistake ever, something good comes from it.

10. When you think the world has turned its back on you, take another look.

11. Always remember the compliments you receive. Forget about the rude remarks."[133]

12. And remember, when life hands you lemons, make some lemonade.

The Bible says we have been created in the image of God. And even when we went astray, Christ came looking for us, giving His life so we can live—forever. That's how precious you are.

You are special. You are loved. And the cross of Calvary testifies to it.

Is God Real to You?

"Recently, third- and fourth-graders at Wheaton Christian Grammar School in Wheaton, Illinois, were asked to complete the following sentence: 'By faith, I know that God is…'. And here is some of what the children said.

- …forgiving, because he forgave in the Bible, and he forgave me when I went in the road on my bike without one of my parents. (Amanda)
- …providingful, because he dropped manna for Moses and the people, and he gave my dad a job. (Brandon)
- caring, because he made the blind man see, and he made me catch a very fast line drive that could have hurt me. He probably sent an angel down. (Paul)
- merciful, because my brother has been nice to me for a year. (Jeremy)
- faithful, because the school bill came, and my mom didn't know how we were going to pay it. Two minutes later, my dad called, and he just got a bonus check. My mom was in tears. (Anonymous)
- sweet, because he gave me a dog. God tells me not to do things that are bad. I need someone like that. (Hannah)"[134]

What this report tells us is that these little kids know that God is not just Someone who was great and amazing to a number of people in the Scriptures. He is Someone who is real in their day-to-day lives.

So the question is, "Is God real in your life?" Or is He just Someone who has shown Himself great and marvelous to some people in the pages of the Bible a long, long time ago?

Christians and Pumpkins

A lady had recently been baptized. One of her co-workers asked what it was like to be a Christian. She was caught off-guard and didn't know what to answer. But when she looked up, she saw a jack-o-lantern on the desk and she answered: "It's like being a pumpkin."

The co-worker asked her to explain. And she did. She said,

"'Well, God picks you from the patch and brings you in and washes all the dirt you may have gotten from the other pumpkins. Then he cuts off the top and scoops out all the yucky stuff. He removes the seeds of doubt, hate, greed, etc. Then He carves you a new smiling face and puts his light inside of you so you can shine for all to see." It is our choice to either stay outside and rot on the vine or come inside and be something new and bright.'"[135]

In the autumn, as we see pumpkins on display at the supermarket or displayed in an empty lot, or jack-o-lanterns with their smiling faces and lights burning bright, let's ask ourselves if we have allowed God to pick us from the vine, washed us clean on the outside, take out the "yucky stuff" inside of us, carve out that new smiling face, and put the light of Jesus inside of us so that we can shine brightly for all to see.

Happy pumpkin celebration for the season!

What Church Are You Looking For?

A man[136] approached a minister and told him he wanted to join his church. The man however added, "But I do have a very busy schedule. I can't be called on for any service, such as teaching in the Sabbath School class, singing in the choir or doing committee work. I won't be available for special projects or to help with setting up chairs or things like that. And I'm afraid I'll be able to go on visitation, as my evenings are all tied up."

The minister thought for a moment, then replied, "I believe you came to the wrong church. The church you're looking for is three blocks down the street, on the right."

The man followed the preacher's directions and soon came to an abandoned, boarded up, closed church building. It was a dead church—gone out of business.

Every year, the Nominating Committee meets and begins calling on church members for leadership and involvement in the various church ministries. How you respond to their call to serve determines whether you are a member of a church that is on its way to being abandoned, boarded up, and closed—a church going out of business. Or hopefully you respond to the call to serve because you are a member of a church that is alive, awake, and zealous to do the task God has commissioned her to do.

A New Way of Tithing

"There was a knock on the door of the hut occupied by a missionary in Africa. Answering the door, the missionary found one of the native boys holding a large fish in his hands.

The boy said, '[Pastor], you taught us what tithing is, so here—I've brought you my tithe.'"

As the missionary gratefully took the fish, he questioned the young lad, "'If this is your tithe, where are the other nine fish?'"

At this, the boy beamed and said, "'Oh, they're still back in the river. I'm now going back to catch them now.'"[137]

Sometimes, we just pay a token tithe—returning only a portion of what we should be giving back to God. At other times, we totally withhold the tithe, using it to meet our supposed material needs—intending, of course, to pay it back at a later time, but that time never happens.

For a change, how about doing something differently—just like the African boy in our story. We can be proactive in our tithe—paying, giving ten per cent of what we desire the Lord to give to us, even before we actually receive it. And then wait and see what God will do, whether He will honor our desires or give us even more than we ever anticipated. There is this promise in Philippians 4:19, "My God shall supply all your need according to his riches in glory by Christ Jesus." And again in Ephesians 3:20: "Now to Him who is able to do exceeding abundantly above all that we ask or think, according to the power that works in us" (NKJV).

Would anyone give this a try? And let me know what happens!

Prescription for Unhappiness

We have talked about a number of suggestions of how we can be happy and successful in life. What I share with you now is geared towards the same purpose, although presented in a reverse way. Looking at it from a different perspective may bring out some gems of thought not readily seen.

The following are ten things we can do if we want to be unhappy in life:

"1. Make little things bother you. Don't just let them, MAKE them!

2. Lose your perspective of things, and keep it lost. Don't put first things first.

3. Get yourself a good worry—one about which you cannot do anything but worry.

4. Be a perfectionist. Condemn yourself and others for not achieving perfection.

5. Be right, always right, perfectly right all the time. Be the only one who is right, and be rigid about your rightness.

6. Don't trust or believe people or accept them at anything but their worst and weakest. Be suspicious. Impute ulterior motives to them.

7. Always compare yourself unfavorably to others, which is the guarantee of instant misery.

8. Take personally, with a chip on your shoulder, everything that happens to you that you don't like.

9. Don't give yourself wholeheartedly or enthusiastically to anyone or to anything.

10. Make happiness the aim of your life instead of bracing for life's barbs through a 'bitter with the sweet' philosophy.[138]

So following the above suggestions guarantees unhappiness. But if you choose happiness, simply break every rule mentioned, and your life can be all that you've ever wanted it to be.

How to Be Perfectly Miserable

In a previous section, we talked about how to be unhappy. This time, I've have something similar. It is entitled "How to be Perfectly Miserable."

"1. Think about yourself.

2. Talk about yourself.

3. Use 'I' as much as possible.

4. Mirror yourself continually in the opinion of others.

5. Listen greedily to what people say about you.

6. Expect to be appreciated.

7. Be suspicious.

8. Be jealous and envious.

9. Be sensitive to slights.

10. Never forgive a criticism.

11. Trust no one but yourself.

12. Insist on consideration and respect.

13. Demand agreement with your own views of everything.

14. Sulk if people are not grateful to you for favors shown them.

15. Never forget a service you may have rendered.

16. Be on the lookout for a good time for yourself.

17. Shirk your duties if you can.

18. Do as little as possible for others.

19. Love yourself supremely.

20. Be selfish."[139]

I think # 20 says it all. "Be selfish." Think about yourself and your own comfort and convenience. Talk about yourself and be the hero of every episode in life. Never be a giving person. Life is all about getting, acquiring, possessing.

These will guarantee you a perfectly miserable existence.

Becoming a Friend and Staying That Way

"In his book, *The Power of Positive Thinking*, Norman Vincent Peale listed these ten rules for becoming the kind of person others like:

1. Learn to remember names.

2. Be a comfortable person so there is no strain in being with you—be an old-shoe, old-hat kind of individual. Be homey.

3. Acquire the quality of relaxed, easy-goingness so that things don't ruffle you.

4. Don't be egotistical. Guard against giving the impression that you know it all. Be natural and normally humble.

5. Cultivate the quality of being interesting so that people will want to be with you and get something of stimulating value from their association with you.

6. Study to get the "scratchy" elements out of your personality.

7. Sincerely attempt to heal, on an honest Christian basis, every misunderstanding you have had and now have. Drain off your grievances.

8. Practice liking people.

9. Never miss an opportunity to say a word of congratulation on anyone's achievement or express sympathy in sorrow or disappointment.

10. Get a deep spiritual experience so that you have something to give people that will help them to be stronger and meet life more effectively. Give strength to people and they will give affection to you."[140]

I would say that if we remembered all these suggestions and put them into practice every day, we would all be friends and stay that way all our lives. In other words, be loving and considerate of others at all times, and they will do the same to you.

Lessons from the Butterfly

Christ's life and ministry on earth were to reveal the nature of God and make known the principles of the kingdom of heaven. And to achieve these, Christ often pointed to the birds of the air, the flowers of the field, and other familiar things in nature. Thus people were continually reminded of these spiritual lessons as they went about their daily round of business.

Nature is God's great lesson book. Next only to the Bible, it speaks of God and His unfathomable wisdom, power, and glory. Even the lowest creatures go about their life cycles in a way that man can learn from.

Just as the caterpillar morphs from an ugly worm to a glorious butterfly, as this insect evolves through its various life stages, it teaches us these life lessons from a butterfly.

"Let go of the past
Trust the future
Embrace change
Come out of your cocoon.

Unfurl your wings
Dare to get off the ground
Ride the breezes.
Savor the flowers.
Put on your brightest colors
Let your beauty show."[141]

So let's learn these lessons from the butterfly. And let our lives be fun and exciting, reflecting the glory of God our Maker.

Six Things to Give

When we think of giving, we usually think of money or things of material value. But these are not necessarily the most meaningful or significant gifts that we can give. In most cases, it is the intangible things that mean a lot to the recipient.

Consider the following lines, based on a quotation from Benjamin Franklin,[142] that show the difference between temporal and eternal values.

> *Let us start blessing others with these gifts. And, as we give, we will also receive of these blessings.*

Six Things to Give

Forgiveness to your enemy,
Tolerance to your friend,
Respect to your father,
Pride to your mother with your good conduct,
Sense of worth to yourself,
And help to the needy.

Let us start blessing others with these gifts. And, as we give, we will also receive of these blessings for the Scriptures say, "The liberal soul shall be made fat: and he that watereth shall be watered also himself" (Prov. 11:25).

Where God Is

"He was just a little boy, on a week's first day.
Wandering home from Bible School,
and dawdling on the way.
He scuffed his shoes into the grass and found a little caterpillar.
He grabbed a fluffy milkweed pod, and blew out all the filler.
A bird's nest in a tree overhead, so wisely placed on high
Was just another wonder that caught his eager eye.
A neighbor watched his zig zag course and hailed him from the lawn,
Asked him where he'd been that day, and what was going on.
'I've been to Bible School,' he said and turned a piece of sod.
He picked up a wiggly worm replying, "I've learned a lot about God.'
'Mm, very fine way,' the neighbor said, 'for a boy to spend his time.'
'If you'll tell me where God is, I'll give you a brand new dime.'
Quick as a flash the answer came! Nor were his accents faint,
'I'll give you a dollar, Mister, if you can tell me where God ain't!'"[143]

> *If we ask the Holy Spirit to give us spiritual discernment, we will see fingerprints of the Creator on the open fields of nature and His signature on every leaf, flower, and bud.*

Oh, that we have the eyes of a child and never lose the wonder of the unaffected mind! If we ask the Holy Spirit to give us spiritual discernment, we will see fingerprints of the Creator on the open fields of nature and His signature on every leaf, flower, and bud.

So God is everywhere and speaks to us all of the time. The question is, "Are we listening?"

I Was a Stranger

"How does your church score? A church newsletter mentioned a man who visited eighteen different churches on successive Sundays. He was trying to find out what the churches were really like [especially in the way they treated visitors. He used a scale to rate the reception he received and he] awarded points on the following basis.

10 for a smile from a worshiper
10 for a greeting from someone sitting nearby
100 for an exchange of names
200 for an invitation to [return]
1,000 for an introduction to another worshiper
2,000 for an invitation to meet the pastor.

On this scale, eleven of the eighteen churches earned fewer than 100 points. Five actually received less than 20. The [results of this private study point to the] conclusion: The doctrine may be biblical, the singing inspirational, the sermon uplifting, but when a visitor finds nobody who cares whether he's there, he's not likely to come back."[144]

And I wondered, if our church had been among those visited, how would we have fared? Would we have scored in the high 3000's, or would we be in the low 100's? When new people visit us, will they want to return when they get the chance; if they are looking for a church home, will they choose to be part of our fellowship? This will depend very much on how we receive them into our midst.

So how about intentionally being warm and friendly to one another, especially to our guests and see how many of them eventually choose to be part of us?

The Serenity Prayer

One of the great frustrations in life is not having it our way. This is a big stressor and is often the cause of conflicts and broken relationships. When everyone wants to have his or her own way, tries to get people to act the way he or she wants them to, and tries to get things done in the way he or she wants them to be done, trouble occurs. We like to impose our will by bossing people around and making ourselves the center around which the whole world must revolve.

The key to serenity and peace of mind is to realize that people are unique and different. The way to have harmony is to accept them for what they are and to know that, in most cases, we need to make the much-needed change.

You may be familiar with the Serenity Prayer that goes like this.

"God grant me the serenity to accept the things I cannot change,
the courage to change the ones I can,
and the wisdom to know the difference."[145]

But here is an interesting twist on this prayer—a variation that is even better because, for the most part, the real problem could be found in us.

"God grant me the serenity to accept the people I cannot change,
the courage to change the ones I can...
and the wisdom to know that one is me."[146]

The Way Up Is the Way Out

"If you put a buzzard in a pen that is 6 feet by 8 feet, and is entirely open at the top, the bird, in spite of its ability to fly, will be an absolute prisoner. The reason is that a buzzard always begins a flight from the ground with a run of 10 to 12 feet. Without space to run, as is its habit, it will not even attempt to fly, but will remain a prisoner for life in a small jail with no top.

The ordinary bat that flies around at night, a remarkably nimble creature in the air, cannot take off from a level place. If it is placed on the floor or flat ground, all it can do is shuffle about helplessly, and, no doubt, painfully, until it reaches some slight elevation from which it can throw itself in the air. Then, at once, it take off like a flash.

A bumblebee, if dropped in an open tumbler, will be there until it dies, unless it is taken out. It never sees the means of escape at the top, but persists in trying to find some way out through the sides near the bottom. It will seek a way where none exists, until it completely destroys itself.

In many ways, we are like the buzzard, the bat ,and the bumblebee. We are struggling about with all our problems and frustrations, never realizing that all we have to do is look up!"[147]

So, the next time you feel overwhelmed on all sides by problems, sin, and temptation, do not be a buzzard, a bat, or a bumblebee. There is a way out, and it is the way up. The Scriptures read, "There hath no temptation taken you but such as is common to man: but God is faithful, who will not suffer you to be tempted above that you are able; but will with the temptation also make a way to escape, that you may be able to bear it" (1 Cor. 10:13).

So there is a way of escape that God has provided from sin and temptation and from the trials and troubles in life. There is a way out and the way up is the way out.

Living in Relationships

"A rather crude and cruel experiment was carried out by Emperor Frederick who ruled the Roman Empire in the thirteenth century. He wanted to know what man's original language was: Hebrew, Greek, or Latin? He decided to isolate a few infants from the sound of the human voice. He reasoned that they would eventually speak the natural tongue of man. Wet nurses who were sworn to absolute silence were obtained, and though it was difficult for them, they abided by the rule. The infants never heard a word—not a sound from a human voice. Within several months they were all dead."[148]

We can live only in relationships. We need each other. The poet John Donne wrote the classic book, *No Man Is an Island*.[149] He says that to be able to really live and enjoy life, we must be immersed in the lives of others. Each man's joys become joys to us, and each man's griefs are our own. So let us defend each other—each man as our brother and each man as our friend.

As much as this is true in society and in the community we live in, it should be even more true in the church—the community of the saints. Jesus said, "…Love one another. as I have loved you" (John 15:12), and John, in his later years, after being with Christ in person for over three years and having lived the longest of all the apostles admonishes, "He that loveth not, knoweth not God, for God is love" (1 John 4:8).

The Rope

"The story tells about a mountain climber, who wanted to climb the highest mountain. He began his adventure after many years of preparation, but since he wanted the glory just for himself, he decided to climb the mountain alone.

The night felt heavy in the heights of the mountain, and the man could not see anything. All was black. It was zero visibility and the moon and the stars were covered by the clouds.

As he was climbing only a few feet away from the top of the mountain, he slipped and fell into the air, falling at a great speed. The climber could only see black spots as he went down, and the terrible sensation of being sucked down by gravity. He kept falling, and, in those moments of great fear, all the good and bad episodes of his life flashed through his mind.

He was thinking about how close death was getting, when all of a sudden he felt the rope tied to his waist pull him very hard.

His body was hanging in mid-air. Only the rope was holding him, and in that moment of stillness, he had no other choice but to scream:

'Help me God!'

All of a sudden, a deep voice from the sky answered:

'What do you want me to do?'

'Save me, God!' the climber replied.

'Do you believe I can save you?'

'Of course I believe you can save me.'

'THEN CUT THE ROPE.'

There was a moment of silence; then the man decided to hold on to the rope with all his strength.

The rescue team found the climber the next morning, frozen to death, his body hanging from the rope around his waist... only 10 feet away from the ground.

What about you: How attached are you to your rope?"[150]

That rope is the symbol of everything that you put your confidence in here in this life. Are you willing to LET GO AND LET GOD?

"God, Speak to Me!"[151]

The man whispered, "God, speak to me,"
And a bird sang,
But the man did not hear.
So the man yelled, "God, speak to me,"
And the thunder rolled across the sky,
But the man did not listen.
The man looked around and said,
"God, let me see You,"
And a star shone brightly,
But the man did not see.
And the man shouted, "God, show me a miracle,"
And a life was born,
But the man did not notice.
So the man cried out in despair,
"Touch me, God, and let me know You are here."
Whereupon, God reached down and touched the man,
But the man brushed the butterfly away and walked on."

God has revealed Himself in many ways to the prophets in the past, and He has made the fullest revelation of Himself in Jesus Christ His Son (Heb. 1:1). But it is still true that He continues to reach down to us and speak to us in many ways.

The question is, "Are we listening?" Do we feel Him when He touches us? Or do we just walk on?

The Spider Web

"A young soldier found himself in a terrible battle during the Scottish Reformation. The enemy was soundly defeating this young man's army. He and his comrades found themselves hastily retreating from the battlefield in defeat, running away in fear for their lives. The enemy gave chase. This young man ran hard and fast, full of fear and desperation, and soon found himself cut off from his comrades-in-arms.

He eventually came upon a rocky ledge containing a cave. Knowing the enemy was close behind and that he was exhausted from the chase, he chose to hide in the cave.... He promised [God] that if he saved him from death, he would devote his life to Him.

When he looked up from his despairing plea for help, he saw a spider beginning to weave its web at the entrance to the cave. As he watched the delicate threads being slowly drawn across the mouth of the cave, the young soldier pondered its irony.

> *When we trust in God, a spider's web is like a stone wall. When we don't trust in God, a stone wall is like a spider's web.*

He thought, 'I asked [God] for protection and deliverance, and He sent me a spider! How can a spider save me?'

His heart was hardened, knowing the enemy would soon discover his hiding place and kill him. Soon he heard the sound of his enemies, who were now scouring the area looking for those in hiding. One soldier with a gun slowly walked up to the cave's entrance. The young soldier inside crouched in fear in the darkness As the enemy cautiously moved forward to enter the cave, he came upon the spider's web, which by now was completely strung across the opening.

He backed away and called out a comrade, 'There can't be anyone in here. They would have had to break this spider's web to enter the cave. Let's move on....'

Years later, this young man made good his promise by becoming a preacher and evangelist. The theme of his preaching was this: 'When we trust in God, a spider's web is like a stone wall. When we don't trust in God, a stone wall is like a spider's web."[152]

Let us all learn a lesson from this story, trusting in God fully for protection and guidance in our lives.

Happy People 1

The *New Scientist* magazine reported a World Values Survey[153] that analyzed the levels of happiness of people living in sixty-five countries around the world. The result is the following list that shows where the happiest people in the world live.

1. Nigeria

2. Mexico

3. Venezuela

4. El Salvador

5. Puerto Rico...

16. United States.

The least happy people live in Russia, Armenia, and Romania.
You will notice that the happiest people, according to this survey, are not necessarily the wealthy who live in abundance and luxury and have all the conveniences of life.
Of course, the factors that make people happy differ from country to country. In the United States, for example, happiness is found in personal success, self-expression, pride, and a high sense of moral esteem. In Japan, however, happiness is found in fulfilling the expectations of family, meeting social responsibilities, and in maintaining high levels of self-discipline, cooperation, and friendliness.
Still, if America is the bastion of Protestant Christianity that claims to have its foundations solely on the Word of God, should not Americans be the happiest people? Did not Jesus say, "...I am come that they might have life, and that they might have it more abundantly" (John 10:10).
Just wondering.

Happy People 2

In the previous section, we talked about a survey, done by *New Scientist* magazine, that described the levels of happiness of people living in 65 countries around the world. And we learned from this study that the happiest people in the world live in Nigeria, Mexico, Venezuela, El Salvador, and Puerto Rico, in that order. The least happy people are the Russians, Armenians, and Romanians. United States came in at #16.

We have noted that the happiest people are not necessarily the wealthy ones. Of course, we understand that the factors that make people happy differ from country to country. In the United States, for example, happiness is found in personal success, self-expression, pride, and a high sense of moral esteem. In Japan, however, happiness is found in fulfilling the expectations of family, meeting social responsibilities, and in maintaining high levels of discipline, cooperation, and friendliness.

In the same article,[154] social scientists give ten suggestions on how people can be happier. These are the following:

1. Get married.
2. Make friends and value them.
3. Desire less.
4. Do someone a good turn.
5. Have faith.
6. Stop comparing your looks to others.
7. Earn more money.
8. Grow old gracefully.
9. Don't worry if you are not a genius.
10. It helps to have a genetic propensity to be happy.

And let me add this: It really helps if one is born again and receives Christ's gift. "These things have I spoken unto you, that my joy might remain in you, and that your joy might be full" (John 15:11).

Best Places to Live in the World

A survey was done by the Mercer Human Resource Consulting Company on the best places to live in the world.[155] In this survey, thirty-nine criteria were used, which ranged from political, social, economic, quality of health, education, transportation services, etc.

The results ranked cities in this order:

1. Vienna, Austria
2. Zürich, Switzerland
3. Munich, Germany
4. Auckland, New Zealand
5. Vancouver, Canada
6. Düsseldorf, Germany
7. Frankfurt, Germany
8. Geneva, Switzerland
9. Copenhagen, Denmark
10. Basil, Switzerland

Luxembourg was the highest-ranked city for personal safety. Milan, Athens, and Rome were the least safe cities in Western Europe. In the United States, Washington, DC, was ranked as #53. Canadian cities were the safest due to strict law enforcement and low crime rates.

The world has its best places but I know of a place that is incomparable in terms of its beauty, glory, peace, and security. It is a place called *heaven*, and Paul, having seen it in all of its majesty says, "...Eye hath not seen, nor ear heard, neither have entered into the heart of man, the things which God hath prepared for them that love him" (1 Cor. 2:9).

I surely would want to go and live there, wouldn't you?

I Wish You Enough

I want to share with you a heart-warming story. It goes like this.

"Recently I overheard a mother and daughter in their last moments together at the airport. They had announced the departure. Standing near the security gate, they hugged and the mother said, 'I love you and I wish you enough.'

The daughter replied, 'Mom, our life together has been more than enough. Your love is all I ever needed. I wish you enough, too, Mom.'

They kissed and the daughter left. The mother walked over to the window where I was seated. Standing there I could see she wanted and needed to cry.

I tried not to intrude into her privacy but she welcomed me in by asking 'Did you ever say goodbye to someone knowing it would be forever?'

'Yes, I have,' I replied. 'Forgive me for asking but why is this a forever goodbye?'

'I am old and she lives so far away. I have challenges ahead and the reality is the next trip back will be for my funeral,' she said.

'When you were saying goodbye, I heard you say 'I wish you enough.' May I ask what that means?'

She began to smile. 'That's a wish that had been handed down from other generations. My parents used to say it to everyone.' She paused for a moment and looked up as if trying to remember it in detail, and she smiled even more.

'When we said, 'I wish you enough' we were wanting the other person to have a life filled with just enough good things to sustain them.' Then turning toward me, she shared the following as if she were reciting it from memory.

'I wish you enough sun to keep your attitude bright no matter how gray the day may appear.

I wish you enough rain to appreciate the sun even more.

I wish you enough happiness to keep your spirit alive and everlasting.

I wish you enough pain so that the smallest joys in life
may appear much bigger.

I wish you enough gain to satisfy your wanting.

I wish you enough loss to appreciate all that you possess.

I wish you enough hellos to get you through the final goodbye.'
She then began to cry and walked away."[156]

The moral of the story is self-evident. I hope you got it. And I also "wish you enough."

God Has Paid It All

Years ago, on a trip to Israel, our Jewish tour guide shared with us the following poem.

"As I was walking down life's highway many years ago,

I came upon a sign that read Heaven's Grocery Store;

When I got a little closer, the doors swung open wide.

And when I came to myself I was standing inside.

I saw a host of angels; they were standing everywhere.

One handed me a basket and said, 'My child shop with care.'

Everything a human being needed was there in that grocery store.

And what you want that you cannot carry with you, you could always come a second time to pick it up.

First I got some Patience. Love was in the same row.

Further down was Understanding—you need that everywhere you go.

I got a box or two of Wisdom and Faith, a bag or two.

And Charity, of course, I would need some of that too.

I couldn't miss the Holy Ghost it was all over the place.

And then some Strength and Courage to help me run this race.

My basket was getting full! But I remembered I needed Grace.

And then I chose Salvation, for Salvation was for free.

I tried to get enough of that to do for you and me.

Then I started to the counter to pay the bill,

For I thought I had everything to do the Master's will.

As I went up the aisle, I saw Prayer and put that in

Because I knew when I stepped outside I would run into sin.

Peace and Joy were plentiful, the last things on the shelf.

Song and Praise were hanging near so I just helped myself.

Then I said to the angel, 'Now how much do I owe?'

He smiled and said, 'Just take them everywhere you go.'

Again I asked, "O really now, how much do I owe?'

'My child,' he said, '"God paid your bill a long, long time ago."'[157]

How true it is that Jesus paid all our debt by His death on the cross. And now we not only have eternal life, but we have every blessing and grace that we need to live a victorious Christian life for Him.

The Power and Patience of Love

Not everyone loved Abraham Lincoln, even when he was the President of the United States. And no one treated him with more contempt than did Edwin Stanton, who denounced Lincoln's policies and called him a "low cunning clown."[158]

Stanton had nicknamed him "the original gorilla" and said that explorer Paul Du Chaillu was a fool to wander about in Africa trying to capture a gorilla, when he could have found one so easily in Springfield, Illinois.[159]

Lincoln said nothing in reply. In fact, he made Stanton his war minister because Stanton was the best man for the job. He treated him with every courtesy. The years wore on.

The night came when an assassin's bullet struck down Lincoln in a theatre. In a room off the side where Lincoln's body was taken, stood Stanton that night. As he looked down on the silent, rugged face of the President, Stanton said through his tears, "There lies the greatest ruler of men the world has ever seen."[160]

Lincoln knew how to deal with his critics and his enemies. He did not fight back. He did not try to get even. He understood the power and the patience of love. And, in the end, he won his enemies to his side.

Jesus says: "...Love your enemies, bless those who curse you, do good to those who hate you, and pray for those who spitefully use you and persecute you" (Matt. 5:44. NKJV).

You Are Blessed

Hurricane Katrina wreaked havoc in Louisiana, leaving in its wake thousands of people who were dead and missing and billions of dollars' worth of property damaged. This was just one more natural calamity that reminds us that we are indeed living in the last days. It also helps us realize how blessed we are as we consider the plight of the disaster victims. Incidentally, I received this message in the mail, and how true it is that we are so blessed in ways we may never even know.

"If you woke up this morning with more health than illness, you are more blessed than the million who won't survive the week.

If you have never experienced the danger of battle, the loneliness of imprisonment, the agony of torture, or the pangs of starvation, you are ahead of twenty million people around the world.

If you attend a church meeting without fear of harassment, arrest, torture, or death, you are more blessed than almost three billion people in the world.

If you have food in your refrigerator, clothes on your back, a roof over your head, and a place to sleep, you are richer than 75% of this world.

If your parents are still married and alive, you are very rare, especially in the United States.

If you hold up your head with a smile and are truly thankful, you re blessed because the majority can, but do not.

If you can hold someone's hand, hug them, or even touch them on the shoulder, you are blessed because you can offer your Maker's healing touch.

If you can read this message, you are more blessed than more than two billion people in the world who cannot read.

You are so blessed in ways you may never know."[161]

"Mister, Are You Jesus?"

Here's a touching story that I want to share. It's so beautiful that I'm giving it as is, from start to finish. It tells us about God's love for us through Jesus's death on the cross, and it challenges each one of us to think about how we ought to live like Him.

"A few years ago a group of salesmen went to a regional sales convention in Chicago. They assured their wives that they would be home in time for Friday night's dinner.

In their rush to catch the plane, one of the salesmen accidentally kicked over a display of apples. Apples flew everywhere. Without stopping or looking back, they all managed to reach the plane in time for their nearly missed boarding. That is, all but one salesman reached the plane. Bob couldn't get out of his head the overturned apples and the look on the poor girl's face who owned it. As they all boarded, Bob paused, took a deep breath, and felt a twinge of compassion for the girl.

He told his buddies to go on without him. As he waved good-bye, he asked one of them to call his wife and explain that he'd be taking a later flight. Bob then returned to the terminal where the apples were strewn all over the terminal floor.

The 16-year-old girl was softly crying, tears running down her cheeks in frustration, as she helplessly groped for her spilled produce. Bob realized she was totally blind! The crowd swirled about her, no one stopping, no one to care for her plight.

The salesman knelt on the floor with her, gathering up the apples. He put them back on the table and helped organize her display. As he did this, he noticed that many of them were battered and bruised; these he set these aside in another basket.

When he had finished, he pulled out his wallet and said to the girl, 'Here, please take this $50 for the damage we did. Are you okay?'

She nodded through her tears. He continued on with, 'I hope we didn't spoil your day too badly.'

As the salesman started to walk away, the bewildered blind girl called out to him, 'Mister...'

He stopped mid-stride and turned and looked into her blind eyes. She continued, 'Are you Jesus?'

And he wondered. Then he slowly walked back to her and then said, 'No, I am nothing like Jesus. He is good, kind, caring, loving, and would never have bumped into your display in the first place.' The girl gently nodded. 'I only asked because I prayed for Jesus to help me gather the apples, and he sent you to help me. Thank you for hearing Jesus, Mister.'

Speechless, the salesman turned from the blind girl and slowly made his way down the terminal corridor to catch the later flight. That question burned and bounced about in his soul: 'Are you Jesus?'

Do people mistake you for Jesus? That's our destiny, is it not? To be so much like Jesus that people cannot tell the difference as we live and interact with a world that is blind to His love, life and grace.

If we claim to know Him, we should live, walk, and act as He would. Knowing Him is more than simply quoting Scripture and going to church. It is actually living the Word as life unfolds day to day.

You are the apple of His eye even though we, too, have been bruised by a fall. He stopped what He was doing and picked us up, you and me, on a hill called Calvary where He paid in full for our damaged fruit."[162]

Let us live like we are worth the price He paid.

How to Stay Young

At our Church Family Night, my wife Ellen did a presentation of research she had done on the topic of "Growing Old Gracefully." She mentioned the basics of staying young that included things like activity, exercise, nutrition, genetics, rest, and getting rid of the toxins in the body.

And then she shared an article entitled, "How to Stay Young Your Whole Life,"[163] written by Dr. Charles Stanley. There were seven recommendations on how we can stay young all of our lives. And to help you remember, they all begin with the letter "L."

1. Keep Learning. When we cease to learn, we get into "rut living," which leads to aging. So don't settle into a boring, predictable routine. Continuing to learn will keep your mind fertile and young.

2. Keep Loving. God created us with the capacity to love. Loving, therefore, is fulfilling the purpose of our creation. Love causes energy to flow into our lives. People who love remain youthful in their spirit for the simple reason that they have anticipation and excitement. They also find ways of looking great all the time, so they can appear attractive to the ones they care most about.

3. Keep Laughing. When we laugh, every cell in our body is affected. The immune system is stimulated and so is our creativity. We also tend to let down our masks and defenses and we become more open and transparent. In other words, we become the real persons that we really are.

   The Scripture says, "A merry heart does good like a medicine, but a broken spirit dries the bones" (Prov. 17:22, NKJV).

   Find friends who make you laugh and hang out with them. And remember that when Christ comes into our lives, there is plenty of reason to rejoice.

4. Keep Laboring. When a person retires and quits working com-

pletely, the brain sends a message to the body: "It's all over!" We stop being challenged and motivated. This is when we begin to age and get old. So find some work to do even when you go into retirement. Psalms 92:14 compares us to strong trees that "...will still bear fruit in old age, they will stay fresh and green." (NIV). And as you continue to be useful, you will stay young.

5. Keep Leaving…your emotional baggage. Too many people live in the past, nurturing old hurts, rejections, and jealousies. They are weighed down by bitterness and haunted by old resentments and hostilities. God never intended His children to live with such burdens.

   If we do not learn to leave the past behind with all its regrets, disappointments, and heartaches, we will age quickly. God wants us to focus our minds on the present and the future, and He is willing to remove our heavy burdens, if we let Him. But we must be willing to stop living in the past. So, let us "Let go and let God."[164]

6. Keep Longing…for better things. Do not give up your dreams or you will start aging. When you are working toward a goal or looking forward to enjoying something you have been dreaming about, you are extremely motivated. And the motivation and anticipation that you experience keeps you young.

   > *So if you no longer have dreams, it's time to start dreaming again. Dream big!*

   So if you no longer have dreams, it's time to start dreaming again. Dream big! And as you dream and work towards your dreams and trust that God will help you realize them, you will discover that you have more energy, more stamina, and more faith. And you will find yourself feeling and looking younger.

7. Keep Leaning…on God. In Proverbs 3:5–6, we read, "Trust in the Lord with all your heart and lean not on your own understanding. In all your ways acknowledge Him, and He shall

direct your paths" (NKJV) When we learn to lean on God for every need—both in good and bad times—we will experience a sense of commitment and joy. We don't have to age because of troubles, trials, or heartaches.

Yes, our body will age. But that doesn't mean we also need to become old in our mind or in our heart. So let us start living today with the assurance and confidence that God will work in our lives and renew our strength.

And may we stay young all our lives!

Life

For about three hours one Wednesday afternoon, millions in America were glued to their television sets as they watched with anxiety a Jet Blue Aircraft Flight # 292, circling the skies of Los Angeles in preparation for an emergency landing. Reports were out that as soon as the plane left Burbank airport for New York, the pilot noticed that one of the nose gears was malfunctioning. Landing the aircraft under this condition could lead to the aircraft bursting into flames. So the pilot determined that the thing to do was to keep flying until the fuel ran out and then go in for an emergency landing at LAX. The strategy worked, and, although the malfunctioning landing gear seemed to have caught fire as the plane taxied on the runway, everything went well. No injury was reported and all 146 passengers and crew got out into safety.[165]

The passengers and crew must have felt they had been given a second chance at life. And I am sure, life to them became all the more precious because of this experience. In fact, all of us experience a second lease on life every day. Every day we live is God's gracious gift to us. The prophet Jeremiah says, "[Thy mercies] they are new every morning: great is Thy faithfulness" (Lam. 3:23).

Consider these words about life.

"Life is an opportunity, benefit from it.

Life is beauty, admire it.

Life is bliss, taste it.

Life is a dream, realize it.

Life is a challenge, meet it.

Life is a duty, complete it.

Life is a game, play it.

Life is costly, care for it.

Life is wealth, keep it.

Life is love, enjoy it.

Life is a mystery, know it.

Life is a promise, fulfill it.

Life is sorrow, overcome it.

Life is a song, sing it.

Life is a struggle, accept it.

Life is a tragedy, confront it.

Life is an adventure, dare it….

Life is too precious, do not destroy it.

Life is life, fight for it.[166]

A Different Kind of Prayer

When the new session of the Kansas State House opened, everyone was expecting the usual generalities. But this is what they heard as Minister Joe Wright began his prayer:

"Heavenly Father, we come before you today to ask for forgiveness and to seek your direction and guidance. We know Your Word says, 'Woe to those who call evil good,' but that is exactly what we have done. We have lost our spiritual equilibrium and inverted our values.

We confess that we have ridiculed the absolute truth of Your Word and called it moral pluralism.

We have worshiped other gods and called it multiculturalism.

We have endorsed perversion and called it an alternative lifestyle.

We have exploited the poor and called it lottery.

We have neglected the needy and called it self-preservation.

We have rewarded laziness and called it welfare.

We have killed our unborn and called it choice.

We have shot abortionists and called it justifiable.

We have neglected to discipline our children and called it building self-esteem.

We have abused power and called it political savvy.

We have coveted our neighbors' possessions and called it ambition.

We have polluted the air with profanity and pornography and called it freedom of expression.

We have ridiculed the time-honored values of our forefathers and called it enlightenment.

Search us, O God, and know our hearts today; try us and see if there be some wicked way in us; cleanse us from every sin and set us free.... Amen!"[167]

Commentator Paul Harvey aired this prayer on his radio program, "The Rest of the Story,"[168] and received a larger response to this program than any other he had ever aired. Requests for copies of the prayer were received from India, Africa, and Korea.

May the sentiments of this prayer sweep over our nation, sparking a revival and reformation so that, once again, America can be "one nation under God."

But it has to start with us.

As you think about yourself, ask God how He can change you and use your God-given skills. Then look for ways to change your community. If everyone would work to change their communities for the better, that would have a positive impact on the country—and from there, even the world.

Making Time for the Things That Really Count

"A long time ago, there was an emperor who told his horseman that he could ride on his horse and cover as much area of land as he likes, then the emperor would give him the area of land that he has covered.

The horseman then quickly jumped onto his horse and rode as fast as possible to cover as much land as he could. He kept riding and riding, whipping the horse to go as fast as possible. When he was hungry or tired, he did not stop because he wanted to cover as much area as possible.

…He had covered a substantial area and he was exhausted and dying. Then he asked himself, 'Why did I work myself so hard to cover so much land? Now I am dying and I only need a small area to bury myself.'"[169]

This story is a story about our lives. Here in America, a land of opportunity, we virtually work ourselves to death in an effort to get as much "land area" (i.e., houses, cars, power, fame) as possible. We neglect our time with our families and our time with God and the church. We don't take time to enjoy the beauty and simple pleasures of life. And then we realize when we get to the end of our journey that we may have achieved wealth, power, and fame but have lost the things that are of eternal value and consequence to us—our families, our character and, most importantly, heaven.

So go ahead. Ride your horse. Stake your land. But don't neglect the things that really count.

Would You Run?

Imagine this scenario....

"Two men covered from head to toe in black and carrying sub-machine guns surprised a 2,000-member congregation one Sunday morning during the service. One of the hooded men proclaimed,

'Anyone willing to take a bullet for Christ, remain where you are.'

Immediately, the choir fled, the deacons fled, and most of the congregation fled.

Out of the 2,000 members, only twenty remained.

The spokesman took off his hood. looked at the preacher, and said, "Okay Pastor, I got rid of all the hypocrites. Now you may begin your service. Have a nice day!' And they left."[170]

Now if this incident had really happened—which is not a far-fetched possibility—and you were part of the congregation, what would you do? Would you run? Or would you stay put, ready to offer your life as a witness to your faith in Christ.

I trust that everyone who enters the sanctuary is a sincere and true worshiper of God. Because this is what God is looking for among those who seek Him.

Life Is a Matter of Priorities

"A professor stood before his philosophy class and had some items in front of him. When the class began, he picked up a very large mayonnaise jar and proceeded to fill it up with golf balls. He then asked the students if the jar was full. They agreed that it was.

The professor then picked up a box of pebbles and poured them into the jar. He shook the jar lightly. The pebbles rolled into the open areas between the golf balls. He then asked the students again if the jar was full. They agreed it was.

The professor next picked up a box of sand and poured it into the jar. Of course, the sand filled up everything else. He once again asked the class if the jar was full. The students responded with a unanimous 'yes.'

The professor then took two [cups of coffee] from under the table and poured the entire contents into the jar, effectively filling the empty space between the sand. The students laughed.

"'Now,' said the professor as the laughter subsided, 'I want you to recognize that this jar represents your life. The golf balls are the important things—your family, your children, your health, your friends and your favorite passions—and if everything else was lost and only they remained, your life would still be full. The pebbles are the other things that matter like your job, your house, and your car. The sand is everything else—the small stuff.

> *We need to line up our priorities and live life the way it should be. And we will find that life can be a beautiful thing!*

'If you put the sand into the jar first,' he continued, 'there is no room for the pebbles or the golf balls. The same goes for life. If you spend all your time and energy on the small stuff you will never have room for the things that are important to you. Pay attention to the things that are critical to your happiness.'

Spend time with your children. Spend time with your parents. Visit with your grandparents. Take your spouse out to dinner. Play another 18 [holes of golf]. There will always be time to clean the house and mow the lawn. Take care of the golf balls first—the things that really matter. Set your priorities. The rest is sand.'

One of the students raised her hand and inquired what the [coffee] represented. The professor smiled and said, 'I'm glad you asked. It just shows that no matter how full your life may seem, there's always room for a couple of [cups of coffee] with a friend.'"[171]

This story and its lesson speak directly to us. And, if we are listening, we need to line up our priorities and live life the way it should be. And we will find that life can be a beautiful thing!

The Parable of the Pencil

This parable has very pointed lessons that merit our special consideration as we look at our responsibilities and our purpose for living.

It is the story of the Pencil and the Pencil Maker. The parable begins in this manner.

"The Pencil Maker took the Pencil aside, just before putting it into the box. 'There are five things you need to know, and you will become the best pencil you can be'.

- '#1. You will be able to do many great things, but only if you allow yourself to be held in Someone's hand.'

- '#2. You will experience a painful sharpening from time to time, but you'll need it to become a better pencil.'

- '#3. You will be able to correct the mistakes you make.'

- '#4. The most important part of you will always be what's inside.'

- '#5. On every surface you are used to write on, you must leave your mark. No matter what the condition, you must continue to write.'

The Pencil understood and promised to remember and went into the box with purpose in its heart."[172]

Now, put yourself in the place of the Pencil and think of the Pencil Maker as God Himself giving instructions to you as He sends you out into the world.

And consider, too, that the only way you can live a vibrant life and serve God effectively is to be held in His hands. This is what He says in John 15:4: "Abide in Me . . . For without Me you can do nothing."

May we all be great pencils, I mean, great Christians for God this year and in the years ahead!

Sharing in the Joys of Creation

Dr. Allan A. Stockdale wrote the following poem to say that God gave us a world unfinished, so that we might share in the joys and satisfaction of creation.

"He left oil in Trenton rock.
He left aluminum in the clay.
He left electricity in the clouds.
He left the rivers unbridged and the mountains untrailed.
He left the forest unfelled, and the cities unbuilt.
He left the laboratories unopened.
He left the diamonds uncut.
He gave us the challenge of raw materials,
Not the satisfaction of perfect, finished things.
He left the music unsung and the dramas unplayed.
He left the poetry undreamed, in order that men and women might not become bored, but engage in stimulating, exciting, creative activities that keep them thinking, working, experimenting, and experiencing all the joys and durable satisfactions of achievement."[173]

What a privilege it is to be a co-creator of God in the things of this world. So let us use our talents and gifts to bring completion and perfection to the world around us. Let it not be said of us that, when our time came, we went to our graves with our music still unsung inside of us.

Moments with God

The following material, though very short and concise, contains good devotional thoughts, and it is something that reminds us how we need to spend every moment, whatever the situation may be, with God.

"Happy moments, praise God.
Difficult moments, seek God.
Quiet moments, worship God.
Painful moments, trust God.
Every moment, thank God."[174]

If everyone did as suggested, we would be bathed in the atmosphere of heaven and people would take notice that—every moment—we are with God.

God Elected You

Every so often, the citizens of this country go to the polls and choose a leader who will be at the helm of the government of the United States of America. America has been beset with so many problems: natural calamities, a huge economic downturn, moral bankruptcy, terrorism, and a host of other issues.

But, in spite of all these turmoils, America remains the world's # 1 superpower that it is supposed to be and will continue to be—thus fulfilling its role according to end-time prophecy. Whoever wins in a U.S. election will have a hand in how soon this country will fulfill its prophetic destiny.

But what we need to remember even more is not the fact that we are trying to choose someone in an election. What is of greater concern to us is to recognize the fact that God has chosen us. The Bible says that He has "…predestined us unto the adoption of children by Jesus Christ to himself, according to the good pleasure of his will to the praise of the glory of his grace, wherein he hath made us accepted in the beloved. In whom we have redemption through his blood, the forgiveness of sins, according to the riches of his grace" (Eph. 1:5–7).

And that's the good news come election day and every day of our lives. Let us therefore choose the destiny that God has given us and allow His Holy Spirit to work out His will in us, guiding and directing us as we live our lives in Him.

A Red-Letter Day in History

On Tuesday, November 4, 2008, the American people went to the polls and made history. The first African-American in the person of Barack Obama was voted into the presidency of the United States, to assume the leadership of this superpower country that is also the acknowledged leader of the Free World.[175]

More than anything though, I was amazed at the way the election process went. Democracy, U.S. style, was demonstrated to the world, and we have shown how a government can be run without hate, prejudice, and bitterness, and how we can live together and resolve our differences in harmony regardless of race, creed, sex, or religion.

Of course, this is what America is according to Bible prophecy. The Good Book describes our nation as a lamb-like beast, a God-fearing nation that finds its strength in its horns—its civil and religious freedoms. But watch out, because it will one day shed its lamb-like characteristics and will speak like a dragon.

Revelation 13:11–17 says, "And I beheld another beast coming up out of the earth; and he had two horns like a lamb, and he spake as a dragon.

And he exerciseth all the power of the first beast before him, and causeth the earth and them which dwell therein to worship the first beast, whose deadly wound was healed.

And he doeth great wonders, so that he maketh fire come down from heaven on the earth in the sight of men,

And deceiveth them that dwell on the earth by the means of those miracles which he had power to do in the sight of the beast; saying to them that dwell on the earth, that they should make an image to the beast, which had the wound by a sword, and did live.

And he had power to give life unto the image of the beast, that the image of the beast should both speak, and cause that as many as would not worship the image of the beast should be killed.

And he causeth all, both small and great, rich and poor, free and bond, to receive a mark in their right hand, or in their foreheads: And that no man might buy or sell, save he that had the mark, or the name of the beast, or the number of his name."

We know that present-day conditions and current events are moving us speedily toward that specific time and place.

Meanwhile, we are glad we still have time to do our God-appointed task. Let us take advantage of the opportunity—while the lamb is continuing to be a lamb. Because when it turns into a dragon, it might be too late.

The Golden Box

Some time ago, "a mother punished her five-year-old daughter for wasting a roll of expensive gold wrapping paper. Money was tight and she became upset when the child used the gold paper to decorate a box to put under the Christmas tree.

Nevertheless, the little girl brought the gift box to her mother the next morning and said, 'This is for you, Momma.'

The mother was embarrassed by her earlier over-reaction, but her anger flared again when she opened the box and found it was empty. She spoke to her daughter in a harsh manner.

'Don't you know, young lady, when you give someone a present there's supposed to be something inside the package?'

The young daughter had tears in her eyes and said, 'Oh, Momma, it's not empty! I blew kisses into it until it was full.'

The mother was crushed. She fell on her knees and put her arms around her little girl, and she begged her forgiveness for her thoughtless anger.

An accident took the life of the child only a short time later, and it is told that the mother kept that gold box by her bed for all the years of her life. Whenever she was discouraged or faced difficult problems, she would open the box and take out an imaginary kiss and remember the love of the child who had put it there.

In a very real sense, each of us, as human beings, has been given a golden box filled with unconditional love and kisses from our children, family, friends, and God. There is no more precious possession anyone could hold."[176]

As we live each day, may we realize that the best gift we can give to, and receive from, our friends and family is love.

And it will be good for us to realize that our loved ones will not be with us forever.

So give them that love today!

The Passion of the Christ

When the movie, "The Passion of the Christ," was released, it got people talking, and it has generated so much interest in the life of Christ and about things spiritual in general.

Reports were made about its overwhelming impact on the viewers—how that minutes into the showing people were heard to be weeping, wailing, confessing sins, asking for forgiveness, and praising God for His grace.

All of a sudden, Jesus was put back into the social consciousness of the world. All of a sudden, people were talking about Jesus's death and sufferings and what they mean.

That presented us with our golden opportunity; when a situation like this occurs, while people are awakening to spiritual things, let us give them the message. There is no better time.

Secrets of a Happy Life

We all want not only to live long lives but also to live happily. It's not just the quantity of life but, more importantly, its quality. And happiness is not something that automatically comes to us, but one that happens when we intentionally try to live happy lives. The following are suggestions on how we can live happy and carefree lives.

"1. Go and have fun in the meadows.

2. Avoid bad habits.

3. Always listen to good advice.

4. Always be alert and then wait. Perhaps what you're looking for will find you.

5. Always be ready for surprises in life.

6. Always look at where you're going.

7. Be determined in achieving your goals.

8. Don't let the situation confuse you.

9. Don't stop your curiosity....

10. And most of all, smile.[177]

Happiness in life is something we need to have. That was one of the reasons Jesus came down to earth. He says in John 10:10: "...I am come that they might have life, and that they might have it more abundantly."

The Day God Visited

In Leo Tolstoy's beautiful story "Where Love Is, God Is Also,"[178] there is an old shoemaker who hears a voice in his deep sleep one night. The voice tells him that, on the very next day, the Lord Jesus will visit him.

Next morning, he begins his work in a spirit of high expectation, as he eagerly awaits the coming of the Lord. But the only visitors he has that day are people in distress, people who need his help.

First, there is an old soldier, shoveling snow in the cold. The old shoemaker takes him in, warms him by the fire, and gives him food.

Next comes a half-frozen, thinly clad woman, carrying her hungry baby in her arms. She needs food and clothing, and the old shoemaker obliges. He gives her a warm coat and some money to buy a shawl.

Then he sees an old woman who is selling apples. She is terribly upset because a boy has tried to steal an apple. The shoemaker knows the boy, and he is able to bring the two together and reconcile them.

This day has not turned out as expected, but the shoemaker has not forgotten the promise of the Lord's visit. Tired now, as he reads his Bible before going to sleep, he hears the same voice from the previous night. This time it says, "I was hungry and you fed Me. I was thirsty and you gave Me drink. I was a stranger, and you invited me into your home. I was naked and you gave me clothing..." (Matt. 25:35–36, NLT).

> *When we show love to these poor and needy folk, we find satisfaction and fulfillment because coming in contact with them brings us in contact with God.*

When God told Moses, "Let them make Me a sanctuary that I may dwell among them" (Exod. 25:8, NKJV), He wasn't saying that churches and cathedrals are the only places where we could find God. True, He has designated certain places where He meets in a special way with His people who come to worship Him. but He can also be found in the back alleys and in prison cells, in sick rooms, and in hovels—because He has said he comes to us in the person of the poor, the suffering, the sick, and the oppressed.

When we show love to these poor and needy folk, we find satisfaction and fulfillment because coming in contact with them brings us in contact with God.

Matthew records a parable told by Jesus that tells what will happen when He comes in glory: "When the Son of man shall come in his glory, and all the holy angels with him, then shall he sit upon the throne of his glory:

And before him shall be gathered all nations: and he shall separate them one from another, as a shepherd divides his sheep from the goats:

And he shall set the sheep on his right hand, but the goats on the left.

Then shall the King say unto them on his right hand, Come, ye blessed of my Father, inherit the kingdom prepared for you from the foundation of the world: For I was an hungered, and ye gave me meat: I was thirsty, and ye gave me drink: I was a stranger, and ye took me in: Naked, and ye clothed me: I was sick, and ye visited me: I was in prison, and ye came unto me.

Then shall the righteous answer him, saying, Lord, when saw we thee an hungered, and fed thee? or thirsty, and gave thee drink?

When saw we thee a stranger, and took thee in? or naked, and clothed thee?

Or when saw we thee sick, or in prison, and came unto thee?

And the King shall answer and say unto them, Verily I say unto you, Inasmuch as ye have done it unto one of the least of these my brethren, ye have done it unto me" (Matt. 25:31-40).

A Prayer

People are different. But most are rational beings who act according to their circumstances and best interests. The reason we become annoyed with other people's behavior is because we are unaware of their particular circumstances. Based on our own circumstances, we probably would characterize someone else's behavior as rude, stupid, or even downright crazy. But if we were to know the other person's circumstances that led to that conduct, we would be more understanding, patient, and forgiving.

Here's a prayer that could help us deal with such day-to-day irritations.

"Heavenly Father,

Help us remember that the [person] who cut us off in traffic last night is a single mother who worked nine hours that day and is rushing home to cook dinner, help with homework, do the laundry, and spend a few precious moments with her children.

Help us to remember that the pierced, tattooed, disinterested young man who can't make change correctly is a worried nineteen-year-old college student, balancing his apprehension over final exams with his fear of not getting his student loans for next semester.

Remind us, Lord, that the scary looking bum, begging for money in the same spot every day (who really ought to get a job!) is a slave to addictions that we can only imagine in our worst nightmares.

Help us to remember that the old couple walking annoyingly slow through the store aisles and blocking our shopping progress are savoring this moment, knowing that, based on the biopsy report she got back last week, this will be the last year that they go shopping together.

Heavenly Father, remind us each day that, of all the gifts you give us, the greatest gift is love. It is not enough to share that love with those we hold dear. Open our hearts not just to those who are close to us, but to all humanity. Let us be slow to judge and be quick to forgive, show patience, empathy, and love."[179]

In Jesus's loving and powerful name, amen.

Happy Thanksgiving, Everyone!

Happiness is a state of mind and not the possession of things that are material and temporal in nature. It is not having what you want but wanting what you have.

It is the same thing with contentment and satisfaction. We are always reminded to, "Count your blessings," but what if we have already done that and are left with nothing more to count?

We can do something else. We can thank God for the things we don't have that we don't want to have. We can be grateful for the things that didn't happen that we didn't want to happen.

How about the accidents that you weren't involved in or the illnesses that you didn't have? You could have been mugged or robbed, but you weren't. Your house didn't burn down even when you left the iron on for five hours. And when you left the garage door up all night, nothing was taken.

"One day on the streets of London, Charles H. Spurgeon was robbed. When he arrived home and told his tale, he said, 'Well, thank the Lord anyway.'

His wife countered, 'Thank the Lord that somebody stole your money?'

'No, my dear,' answered her husband....

'First, I'm thankful the robber just took my money, not my life.'

'Secondly, I'm thankful I had left most of our money at home, and he really didn't rob me of much.'

'Thirdly, I'm thankful to God that I was not the robber.'"[180]

A happy Thanksgiving weekend to everyone!

Reverse or Proper Proportion of Thanksgiving?

In his book, *Table Talk*, Martin Luther says, "The greater God's gifts and works, the less they are regarded."[181] His statement seems to imply that our degree of thanksgiving in life is in reverse proportion to the amount of blessings we receive.

This would seem to say that a hungry man is more thankful for a morsel of bread that is given him than a rich man is for his heavily laden table. Or that a lonely woman in a nursing home will appreciate a visit more than a popular woman who has a party thrown in her honor. A Russian who gets a copy of the Holy Scriptures after seventy-five years of state-imposed atheism is more thankful for his little book than we are for all the Christian books and magazines and translations that overflow our shelves.

Many of us take so many blessings for granted because they are so freely accessible and abundant to us—like the air we breathe, water for our drinking and bathing needs, the roof over our heads, warm beds and blankets on cold, wintry nights, educational and recreational opportunities, health, food, and so many other things in life.

Most of these blessings we take for granted because they are so abundant and are so readily available at our beck and call. But for so many millions in other parts of the world, these blessings are things that they can only dream of. And it would seem, from Luther's statement, that less fortunate people are more grateful for their meager blessings than we are for our more abundant supplies.

If the Holy Spirit is working in our lives, this pattern of giving thanks would be reversed. And as evidence of the Holy Spirit's work, we would be thanking God in proper proportion, not in reverse proportion, for all the gifts and blessings that we receive from His beneficent hands.

Why the Nine Did Not Return

While Jesus was on His way to Jerusalem from Galilee, ten lepers came to Him, begging for mercy. The Scripture says that He had compassion on them and told them to go show themselves to the priest. Taking Jesus at His word, they went and, on their way, they were healed. Their horrible condition was cured and whatever ravages the terrible disease had had on their bodies were gone.

One of the ten came back, praising God and thanking Jesus for His healing. Jesus was glad someone came to give thanks. But, at the same time, He was sad that only one of them returned to say, "Thank you." His eyes peered into the distance, asking, "Were not ten healed? Where are the nine?" (Luke 17:11-19, MSG).

Someone wondered why the nine did not return to give thanks for their healing. And the following reasons are suggested.

"1. One waited to see if the cure was real.

2. One waited to see if it would last.

3. One said he would see Jesus later.

4. One decided that he had never had leprosy.

5. One said he would have gotten well anyway.

6. One gave glory to the priests.

7. One said, 'O, well, Jesus didn't really do anything.'

8. One said, 'Any rabbi could have done it.'

9. One said, 'I was already much improved.'"[182]

The above possible reasons why the nine lepers who were healed didn't return to give thanks describe the attitude of the naturally ungrateful human heart. It shows how we really are—we are unappreciative of what God has done for us and unthankful for the countless blessings we receive from His beneficent hand. We are proud, self-sufficient, indifferent, apathetic, arrogant, and downright ungrateful.

God does not need our gratitude to feel good or happy. But just the same He is grieved when we are ungrateful and fail to acknowledge His blessings. He looks for us whenever we neglect to give Him our thanks.

Do we keep Him waiting to receive the thanks and gratitude that He deserves?

Giving Thanks

This poem by an unknown author was set to music by J. H. Fillmore in this old-time hymn entitled, "Thanksgiving."[183]

"For the hay and the corn and the wheat that is reaped,
For the labor well done, and the barns that are heaped,
For the sun and the dew and the sweet honeycomb,
For the rose and the song and the harvest brought home --
Thanksgiving! Thanksgiving!

For the trade and the skill and the wealth in our land,
For the cunning and strength of the workingman's hand,
For the good that our artists and poets have taught,
For the friendship that hope and affection have brought—
Thanksgiving! Thanksgiving!

For the homes that with purest affection are blest,
For the season of plenty and well-deserved rest,
For our country extending from sea unto sea;
The land that is known as the 'Land of the Free'
Thanksgiving! Thanksgiving!"

Thanksgiving is the time of year when we are reminded about how we should ever be thankful for our blessings.

So, as we count our blessings, naming them one by one, may our hearts indeed fill with gratitude to God from whom all blessings flow.

His Word says, "Every good gift and every perfect gift is from above, and comes down from the Father of lights, with whom there is no variation or shadow of turning" (James 1:17, NKJV).

If You Never

Trials and reversals of fortune are common occurrences in life. They will either discourage us in our Christian journey or spur us in our spiritual experience, making us soar to greater heights like a kite when loosed by the wind. It all depends on what attitude or mindset we take about life in general and where we place God in it.

When Paul asked God to remove a "thorn in the flesh" (2 Cor. 12:7), that he thought was hampering his ministry and devotion to Him, God decided not to grant Paul's request but instead chose to provide him with strength so that he was able to endure it and to realize his total dependence on Him. God said, "My grace is sufficient for you, for My strength is made perfect in weakness" (2 Cor. 12:9).

Life's trials and difficulties come to remind us of our total dependence on God. Indeed, these things come to us so that we can feel our need of Him

> *When life's trials and difficulties come, let us know that they only remind us of our total dependence on God.*

The following poem by an anonymous author deals more with this thought.

And God Said If...

If you never felt pain,
Then how would you know that I'm a Healer?
If you never went through difficulties,
Then how would you know that I'm a Deliverer?
If you never had a trial,
Then how could you call yourself an overcomer?
If you never felt sadness,
Then how would you know that I'm a Comforter?
If you never made a mistake,

Then how would you know that I'm forgiving?
If you never were in trouble,
Then how would you know that I will come to your rescue?
If you never were broken,
Then how would know that I can make you whole?
If you never had a problem,
Then how would you know that I can solve them?
If I gave you all things,
Then how would you appreciate them?
If I never corrected you,
Then how would you know that I love you?
If your life was perfect,
Then what would you need Me for?[184]

So when life's trials and difficulties come, let us know that they only remind us of our total dependence on God.

Thank You, Lord

One of the keys to a happy and successful Christian life is a grateful heart. No matter what your circumstances are, if you trust in God and know that God is guiding and providing for your life, you will not need to worry or fret. You may feel inconvenienced at times, but you know that God is letting you go through some circumstances because He has a wonderful plan for you that will be for your permanent good. Does not the Bible say that "...all things work together for good to them that love God..." (Rom. 8:28)?

The apostle Paul, who lived a victorious Christian life, further says that he learned this lesson: "...in whatever state I am, to be content" (Phil. 4:11, NKJV). This is the key to happy, Christian living.

The following poem, "Everyday Thanksgiving," can help us maintain a happy state of mind despite the troubles and bumps we experience on our journey.

> Even though I clutch my blanket and growl when the alarm rings. Thank you, Lord, that I can hear. There are many who are deaf.

> Even though I keep my eyes tightly closed against the morning light as long as possible. Thank you, Lord, that I can see. There are many who are blind.

> Even though I huddle in my bed and put off the effort of rising. Thank you, Lord, that I have the strength to rise... There are many who are bedridden.

> Even though the first hour of my day is hectic, when socks are lost, toast is burned, tempers are short, Thank you, Lord, for my family. There are many who are lonely.

> Even though our breakfast table never looks like the picture in magazines and the menu is at times unbalanced, thank you, Lord, for the food we have. There are many who are hungry.

Even though the routine of my job often is monotonous. Thank you, Lord, for the opportunity to work. There are many who have no job.

Even though I grumble and bemoan my fate from day to day and wish my circumstances were not modest. Thank you, Lord, for the gift of life.[185]

Look back and thank God.

Look forward and trust God.

Look around and serve God.

Look within and find God.

So have a grateful heart and you will have a happy and successful Christian life.

When to Say "Thank You" to God

The Thanksgiving season is one of my favorite times of the year in America. It is a time for family reunions, holiday feasts, turkey and stuffing, Indian corn, and pumpkin pies. And, of course, people are generally more good-natured as they get into the spirit of thanksgiving.

As we count our blessings and say our prayer of thanksgiving to God because "every good gift and every perfect gift is from above and cometh down from the Father of lights, in whom there is no variableness, neither shadow of turning" (James 1:17), I want to share with you a prayer that is worth modeling our prayers after during this special time.

"Dear God:

I want to thank You for what You have already done. I am not going to wait until I see results or receive rewards;

I am thanking You right now.

I am not going to wait until I feel better or things look better;

I am thanking You right now.

I am not going to wait until people say they are sorry or until they stop talking about me;

I am thanking You right now.

I am not going to wait until the pain in my body disappears;

I am thanking You right now.

I am not going to wait until my financial situation improves;

I am thanking You right now.

I am not going to wait until the children are asleep and the house is quiet;

I am thanking You right now.

I am not going to wait until I get promoted at work or until I get a job;

I am thanking You right now.

I am not going to wait until I understand every experience in my life that has caused me pain or grief;

I am going to thank You right now.

I am not going to wait until the journey gets easier or the challenges are removed;

I am thanking You right now.

I am thanking You because I am alive.

I am thanking You because I made it through the day's difficulties.

I am thanking You because I have walked around the obstacles.

I am thanking You because I have the ability and the opportunity to do more and do better.

I'm thanking You because You haven't given up on me...."[186]

Happiness is Now

Happiness is as elusive as a butterfly. The more we try to catch it, the farther it goes away from us. . .

And so we resign ourselves into saying that at some point in time, somewhere in the future, we will ultimately find happiness.

"We convince ourselves that life will be better after we get married, have a baby, then another.

Then we are frustrated that the kids aren't old enough and we'll be more content when they are.

After that, we're frustrated that we have teenagers to deal with. We will certainly be happy when they are out of that stage.

We tell ourselves that our life will be complete when our spouse gets his or her act together, when we get a nicer car, when we are able to go on a nice vacation, or when we retire.

The truth is, there's no better time to be happy than right now.

If not now, when?

Your life will always be filled with challenges. It's best to admit this to yourself and decide to be happy anyway."

Happiness is the way. So treasure every moment that you have. And treasure it more because you find that you will enjoy it more when you share it with someone special, special enough to spend your time with."[187187]

Truly, happiness is not in yesterday when things were simpler and less complicated. It's not tomorrow when our family or friends can all love each other. Or when our goals have been realized and our dreams fulfilled. It is today because happiness is not so much found in some memory of the past or in a hope of the future. It's not so much in the destination. It is actually in the journey, in the here and now.

Be Thankful, Always

November is Thanksgiving Month. This is not to say it is the only month in which we should have the spirit of thanksgiving and gratitude. But it is to remind us of the importance of a life of thanksgiving in spite of the disappointments and trials that sometimes come upon us.

This poem, "The Alphabet" encourages us to be grateful all our lives until we get to heaven where no one will ever be sad.

"**A**lthough things are not perfect
Because of trial or pain
Continue in thanksgiving
Do not begin to blame
Even when the times are hard
Fierce winds are bound to blow
God is forever able.

Hold on to what you know
Imagine life without His love
Joy would cease to be!
Keep thanking Him for all the things
Love imparts to thee
Move out of "Camp Complaining."

No weapon that is known
On earth can yield the power
Praise can do alone
Quit looking at the future
Redeem the time at hand
Start every day with worship.

To "thank" is a command
Until we see Him coming
Victorious in the sky
We'll run the race with gratitude

'**X**alting God most high
Yes, there'll be good times and yes some will be bad, but…
Zion waits in glory…where none are ever sad!"[188]

May you be thankful always, whatever your circumstances.

Happy Thanksgiving Day to All!

To many, Thanksgiving is a favorite time of the year. For one thing, Thanksgiving time is family time. Perhaps more than any holiday of the year, this is the day when children want to be with their parents and when parents want all their children home. This also explains why Thanksgiving Day is the most traveled holiday of the year. Besides, this is a nice holiday because in addition to the family fun and togetherness, there is no pressure from shopping and holiday gift-giving, as in other holidays.

The problem with this holiday, and other holidays for that matter, is that in the very act of celebration, we oftentimes lose its meaning and purpose. True, we might make an effort to dress like pilgrims, eat turkey, fish, squash, corn, and pumpkin pie, but that's about it.

Do we even think about how the pilgrims braved the sea, the harsh winter, and the threat of Indians in the New World—all because they wanted to escape religious persecution in the Old World and desired to establish a country and a government where each one was free to worship God according to the dictates of his or her own conscience? So if this is what Thanksgiving is all about, what are we doing to show appreciation for our civil and religious freedoms? I was just wondering....

The Pilgrims Came

> The pilgrims came across the sea,
> And never thought of you and me;
> And yet it's very strange the way,
> We think of them Thanksgiving Day.
> We tell their story, old and true
> Of how they sailed across the blue;
> And found a new land to be free,
> And built their homes quite near the sea.
>
> Every child knows well the tale
> Of how they bravely turned the sail;
> And journeyed many a day and night,
> To worship God as they thought right."[189]

Have a meaningful Thanksgiving Day celebration!

The Shipwreck

"The only survivor of a shipwreck was washed up on a small, uninhabited island. He prayed feverishly for God to rescue him, and every day he scanned the horizon for help, but none seemed forthcoming. He eventually managed to build a little hut out of driftwood to protect him from the elements, and to store his few possessions.

One day, after scavenging for food, he arrived home to find his little hut in flames, the smoke rolling up to the sky. It was just more than he could take. He was stunned with grief and anger. 'God, how could you do this to me!'

But the next day, he woke to the sound of a ship approaching the island to rescue him. 'How did you know I was here?'" asked the weary man of his rescuers. 'We saw your smoke signal,' they replied."[190]

It is hard to maintain our faith stance and spiritual composure when we are doing the best we can to serve the Lord and follow him in the path of self-denial and sacrifice and still experience fierce trial and suffering. But Paul, in his letter to the Romans says, "And we know that all things work together for good to those who love God, to those who are the called according to His purpose" (Rom. 8:28, NKJV).

So don't get discouraged. When things begin to go against you, be assured that God is working in your life, even in the midst of pain and suffering. And next time you see your little hut burning to the ground, be ready for a miraculous deliverance—it could just be a smoke signal summoning God's grace for your particular need.

The Ant and the Contact Lens[191]

This true story was told by Josh and Karen Zarandona. Brenda was a young woman who was invited to go rock climbing. Although she was very sacred, she went with her group to a tremendous granite cliff. In spite of her fear, she put on the gear, took hold of the rope, and started up the face of the rock.

She got to a ledge where she could get a breather. As she was hanging on there, the safety rope snapped against Brenda's eye and knocked out her contact lens. So here she was, on a rock ledge, with hundreds of feet below her and hundreds of feet above her. Of course she looked and looked, hoping it had landed on the ledge, but it just wasn't there. Here she was, far from home, her sight now blurry. She was desperate and began to get upset, so she prayed to the Lord to help her find it.

When she got to the top, a friend examined her eye and her clothing for the lens, but there was no contact lens to be found. She sat down despondent, with the rest of the party, waiting for the rest of them to make it up the face of the cliff.

She looked out across range after range of mountains, thinking of the Bible verse that says: "The eyes of the Lord run to and fro throughout the whole earth...." She thought, 'Lord, you can see all these mountains. You know every stone and leaf, and You know exactly where my contact lens is. Please help me.'

Finally, they walked down the trail to the bottom. There was a new party of climbers just starting up the face of the cliff. One of them shouted out, 'Hey, you guys! Anybody lose a contact lens?' Well, that would be startling enough, but you know why the climber saw it? An ant was moving slowly across the face of the rock, carrying it!

Brenda told me that her father is a cartoonist. When she told him the incredible story of the ant, the prayer, and the contact lens, he drew a picture of the ant lugging that contact lens with the words, 'Lord, I don't know why you want me to carry this thing. I can't eat it, and it's awfully heavy. But if this is what You want me to do, I'll carry it, I will.'"

It would be nice for us to pray this prayer, "God, I don't know why you want me to carry this load. I can see no good in it and it's awfully heavy. But if you want me to carry it, I will."

Are You Saving for Eternity?

Jesus said, "What shall it profit a man, if he shall gain the whole world, and lose his own soul? Or what shall a man give in exchange for his soul?" (Mark 8:36–37).

Every day, we are faced with the pressures of work. And it is not just work to be able to live, but it is work to be able to live in as comfortable a manner as we can imagine. The things of this life simply bewitch us, and there is no end to accumulating these material possessions and worldly goods.

What is tragic is the fact that, at times, our time is so consumed by this effort that there is nothing left for the things of eternity. Service to God and ministry to our fellowmen no longer figure into our consciousness as motivating factors.

> *Service to God and ministry to our fellowmen no longer figure into our consciousness as motivating factors.*

An unknown author penned the following words which reminds us about how we must work.

"Out of this life I shall never take,
Things of silver and gold I make.
All that I cherish and hoard away,
After I leave, on the earth must stay.
Though I have toiled for a painting rare,
To hang on the wall, I must leave it there;
Though I call it mine and I boast of its worth,
I must give it up when I quit the earth.
All that I gather and all that I keep,
I must leave behind when I fall asleep.
And I often wonder what I shall own
In that other life when I pass alone....
Shall the great Judge learn when my task is through,
That my spirit had gathered some riches, too?
Or shall at the last it be mine to find
That all I'd worked for, I'd left behind."[192]

Getting Bold for Christ

"The new president of a bank made an appointment with his predecessor to seek some advice. He began, 'Sir, as you well know, I lack a great deal of the qualifications you already have for this job. You have been very successful as president of this bank, and I wondered if you would be kind enough to share with me some of the insights you have gained from your years here that have been the keys to your success.'

The older man looked at him with a stare and replied: 'Young man, two words: Good Decisions.'

The young man responded, 'Thank you very much, sir, but how does one come to know which is the good decision?'

'One word, young man: Experience.'

'But how does one get experience?'

'Two words, young man: Bad Decisions.'"[193]

In day-to-day living, we have God's Word to guide us in making morally right decisions. But there are times when the things we decide don't have anything to do with morality. A lot of the time, it's about deciding between the good and the better or between the better and the best.

We should never hesitate about making up our minds. Let us exercise this prerogative. This is what makes us distinct as individuals and what separates us from God's lower creation. It makes life more meaningful and serving the Lord more exciting. Not making decisions because we are scared we might make a mistake reminds me of an amusing little poem:

> "There was a very cautious man,
> Who never laughed or played.
> He never risked, he never tried,
> He never sang or prayed!
> And when one day he passed away,
> His insurance was denied,
> For since he never really lived,
> They claimed he never really died!"[194]

God Has a Need for You

At some time towards the end of the year, church officers are chosen for the new year. With the work that needs to be done, there is a need for many volunteers and workers for the various ministries and responsibilities. So the Nominating Committee gives members a call. Will you accept or decline the invitation to serve? Will you be willing to commit your time, your talents, your treasure, and your body temple to advance the cause of God, or will you "lie low," choosing to be excused and basically live for yourself this coming year?

Here's a poem that is so appropriate and one that can help us decide what we will do with our lives this coming year.

> "The Lord had a job for me,
> But I had so much to do.
> I said, 'You'll get somebody else,
> Or wait till I get through.'
> I don't know how the Lord made out,
> No doubt He got along,
> But I felt kind of sneaking like,
> I knew I had done God wrong.
> One day I needed the Lord,
> Needed Him right away;
> But He never answered me at all,
> And I could hear Him say,
> Down in my accusing heart;
> 'Child of Mine, I've got too much to do
> You get somebody else
> Or wait till I get through!'
> Now when the Lord has a job for me
> I never try to shirk.
> I drop what I have on my hands
> And do the Lord's good work.
> And my affairs can run along
> Or wait till I get through,
> For nobody else can do the work
> That God's marked out for you!"[195]

Scenic Wonders of Scandinavia and Russia

Our travels have taken us to the northern parts of the globe—through the countries of Scandinavia (Denmark, Sweden, Norway, and Finland) and Russia. It was a unique and wonderful experience—sailing on the fjords of Norway, beholding its many majestic waterfalls, its lush and fertile valleys, its towering mountains, and the calm and serene waters of its many lakes. I was impressed and quite amused at the way Norwegians take pride in the beauty of their land. I saw a poster that read, "If God had a second home, it would be Norway!"

We have also been awed at the many wonders of man's inventions—the many canals of beautiful Stockholm (Sweden) with their clear blue waters and those of St. Petersburg (Russia, the Venice of the North). St. Petersburg—with its many magnificent palaces and priceless collections of art, sculptures, and paintings by the masters in its many museums—rivals, if not exceeds, Paris and the palace of Versailles which czar Peter the Great, its founder and builder, supposedly used as model.

On our final Sabbath there, we had the opportunity to worship with our small group of Adventist believers in the city of Helsinki, Finland. It was a pleasant surprise when we stopped in unannounced at the place where our brethren met for worship.

As soon as I stepped inside the room where worship was going to be held, I was greeted by a "Kumusta po kayo ("How are you? in the Tagalog language), Pastor!"

The pastor of our international group there was a Filipino young man who graduated from the Adventist University of the Philippines, a batchmate (fellow graduate) of Pastor Ariel Roxas, our youth pastor at Central Filipino Church. Obviously, Pastor Roxas alerted his friend about a possible visit of our group as I mentioned to him Helsinki was part of our itinerary. And the two were friends who continued to be in touch with each other. They received us with so much warmth and hospitality and I was given the special privilege of sharing the Word of God with them during the worship hour.

We are grateful to God for His protection while we flew in the air, rode the bus or cruised the North, Norwegian, and the Baltic seas. He had us safely in His care.

And many thanks to all of you for your prayers for our safety and health during the trip.

Christmastime

It's Christmastime and all over the land the air is filled with the feeling and excitement of Christmas as we celebrate the birth of our Savior long ago in the little town of Bethlehem. As we rejoice in this most wonderful gift that heaven bestowed on the human race. We also remember feelings of love, joy, and peace, as we recall experiences we have had in our celebration of Christmas through the years.

Barbara Laughlin wrote a poem, "Christmas is a Time—for Sharing" that reminds us that Christmastime is also a time for sharing, for caring, for giving, and for remembering, for love and joy and peace.

"Old stories passed down through the years,
"What grandpa did one Christmas eve,"
Had you laughing through your tears.
Christmas is a time—for caring
About your family, neighbors, and friends;
Lending a hand to others in need
Before the season ends.
Christmas is a time—for giving
Presents that come from your heart;
Watching the children, hearing their laughter
As the packages are torn apart.
Christmas is a time— for peace
When soldiers lay aside their guns;
And raise a glass to peace and good will
To every father and every son.
Christmas is a time—for remembering
Family not with us on Christmas morn;
And why people everywhere celebrate
The night our Savior was born."[196]

The Colors of Christmas

As December sets in, we begin to experience the sights and sounds of Christmas. We see and hear so many ways people express themselves as they celebrate this most popular holiday of the year. And although we don't know exactly when Jesus was born, it is still a special blessing to be able to think of His birth and thank Him for coming into our world to save us from sin.

As we begin to celebrate the wonderful event of Christ's birth, let us remind ourselves to be focused on Him and not be sidetracked by the very activities celebrating His birth. Let us tell ourselves and the little ones that Christmas is all about Him, and not about parties and Christmas trees and lights and presents. And whatever we do to celebrate His birth points to Him who is the reason for the season. The way Christmas is celebrated with some people exploiting the event for its commercial value, we now hear more about that than we hear about the Creator of the universe leaving His home in glory and coming to be born as a helpless baby in this world lost and fallen in sin. The true significance of this event has been lost in the minds of people. Christmas is parties and shopping and gifts without a real focus on the reason for this season.

> *Why don't we celebrate Christmas by appreciating the lovely colors around us and see in each color the blessings that Jesus came to bring.*

In the following poem, the way people do Christmas does not have to be a distraction. We can turn it into a positive thing. If you haven't noticed it yet, December is probably the most colorful month of the year. Why don't we celebrate Christmas by appreciating the lovely colors around us and see in each color the blessings that Jesus came to bring.

Here is **"The Colors of Christmas"** poem.

"The colors of Christmas are bright and they're true.
They tell of God's great love for me and for you.
Blue is the sky where the angels appeared.
as they sang. 'Peace on earth' to the shepherds who feared.
Silver is for the bright Christmas star
Which guided the wise men from countries afar.
Gold tells of their gifts for the Baby that day,
who they found in a manger, asleep on the hay.
Purple for suffering and death on a hill.
Red is the blood which Jesus did spill.
Green shows that Jesus arose from the dead
And saved us and freed us, just as He said."[197]

When we turn to these thoughts each time we see a brightly colored Christmas décor, our Christmas experience will become more meaningful and blessed.

Let us ever remember that Jesus came, choosing to give up His riches so that through His poverty we might become rich. Paul said, "For ye know the grace of our Lord Jesus Christ, that, though he was rich, yet for your sakes he became poor, that ye through his poverty might be rich" (2 Cor. 8:9).

So have a merry, colorful Christmas this year!

Christmas Is About Leaving Home

Most of us have wonderful memories of Christmases past. And I am sure some of them go back to our early childhood while we were growing up and celebrating the season with our families. We like to perpetuate this tradition, and so we take a vacation from work and school just so that we can enjoy the holidays with our loved ones.

And are you familiar with the song, "I'll be home for Christmas"?[198] The singer tries to get home for the holidays, but when it becomes physically impossible, he resigns himself by singing the last line of the song, "I'll be home for Christmas, if only in my dreams."

George Murray, missionary and president of Columbia International University, wrote about the many Christmases he and his wife spent abroad. He wrote about how lonely they felt. How strange the foreign holiday customs felt. How homesick they were for family, friends, and simple, familiar pleasures like pumpkin pie.

"Then one day as George was meditating on the meaning of Christmas, it hit him: Christmas isn't about going home. It's all about leaving home. That's what Jesus did. He left the comfort and security of His heavenly home to come to this sin-filled world. He was obeying His heavenly Father. He was representing God to this world."[199]

He said, "For I have come down from heaven, not to do My own will, but the will of him who sent me" (John 6:38, NKJV). "Behold, I have come… to do Your will, O God" (Heb 10:7, NAS).

May the Christmas story inspire us to leave home—leave our comfort zones and represent God in this sin-filled world.

Finding Christ and Worshiping Him This Christmas

Much too often, Christ—the reason for the season—gets lost in all the celebrations at Christmastime. The holidays that have been set up to remember His birth have become so big that the very essence of His person and His mission upon earth have become buried in all the hoopla and frenzy of it all.

But we need not despair, and this ought not be a reason to stop celebrating the holiday. It is much better to realize where the problem lies and make it our mission to look for Christ at Christmastime and—finding Him—to fall down on our knees to worship Him.

This beautiful poem, **"Can This Be Christmas?"** written by M. R. DeHaan, M.D., speaks about this point:

> What's all this hectic rush and worry?
> Where go these crowds who run and hurry?
> Why all the lights—the Christmas trees?
> The jolly "fat man," tell me please!
>
> Why, don't you know? This is the day
> For parties and for fun and play;
> Why this is Christmas!
>
> So this is Christmas, do you say?
> But where is Christ this Christmas day?
> Has He been lost among the throng?
> His voice drowned out by empty song.
>
> No. He's not here—you'll find Him where
> Some humble soul now kneels in prayer,
> Who knows the Christ of Christmas.
>
> But see the many aimless thousands
> Who gather on this Christmas Day,
> Whose hearts have never yet been opened,
> Or said to Him, "Come in to stay."

In countless homes the candles burning,
In countless hearts expectant yearning
For gifts and presents, food and fun,
And laughter till the day is done.

But not a tear of grief or sorrow
For Him so poor He had to borrow
A crib, a colt, a boat, a bed
Where He could lay His weary head.

I'm tired of all this empty celebration,
Of feasting, drinking, recreation;
I'll go instead to Calvary.

And there I'll kneel with those who know
The meaning of that manger low,
And find the Christ—this Christmas.

I leap by faith across the years
To that great day when He appears
The second time, to rule and reign,
To end all sorrow, death, and pain.

In endless bliss we then shall dwell
With Him who saved our souls from hell,
And worship Christ—not Christmas![200]

Have a merry Christmas everyone, as you find the Christ of Christmas!

Looking for Christ at Christmas

Christmas is unarguably the happiest time of the year. The Christmas spirit is such that, when the season comes around, people are more loving, more giving, and more kind to one another. The parties, the decorations, the lights, the giving and receiving of gifts, and everything that goes with the celebration make Christmas a most memorable time of the year and something that we look forward to every time.

> *And no Christmas can be truly Christmas unless the celebration is held in His honor.*

But happy as this occasion may be, its meaning can only be realized when the celebration focuses on Jesus who is the reason for Christmas. After all, it is a celebration of His birth. He is the reason for the season. And no Christmas can be truly Christmas unless the celebration is held in His honor.

So, as we once again join the Christian world in celebrating the birth of our Savior, may we look for Him and may we find him amid all the excitement and the hustle and bustle of our Christmas celebrations.

If You Look for Me at Christmas

If you look for me at Christmas
you won't need a special star.
I'm no longer only in Bethlehem,
I'm right there where you are.
You may not be aware of Me
amid the celebrations.
You'll have to look beyond the stores
and all the decorations.
But if you take a moment
from your list of things to do
And listen to your heart,

you'll find I'm waiting there for you.
You're the one I want to be with,
you're the reason that I came,
And you'll find Me in the stillness
as I'm whispering your name."[201]

Love,
Jesus

He wants to be with us. May we connect with Him in a special way this Christmas.

A Heads Up for Christmas Gift-givers

The Christmas season is just upon us. Christmas carols fill the air and, all around, it's beginning to look a lot like Christmas. Already, parties are beginning to happen and programs and shows featuring the nativity and birth of Jesus are getting their share of the spotlight.

And, of course, the shopping for gifts to impress and show appreciation for loved ones has begun. Some Christmas shoppers are smart. They shop months before the holiday season comes around. And this is great, as they are able to avoid the long lines, the rush, and the stress that usually accompany lastminute holiday shoppers.

While you can do something to improve your Christmas gift-giving tradition, it is far more important to work on the quality and lasting effects of your gifts.

In the book, *Growing Strong*, Charles Swindoll, talks about certain gifts we could give that far outweigh the value of material gifts no matter how expensive they may be.

He says,

"Some gifts you can give this Christmas are beyond monetary value:

Mend a quarrel,

Dismiss suspicion,

Tell someone, 'I love you.'

Give something away—anonymously.

Forgive someone who has treated you wrong.

Turn away wrath with a soft answer.

Visit someone in a nursing home.

Apologize if you were wrong.

Be especially kind to someone with whom you work.

Give as God gave to you in Christ, without obligation, or announcement, or reservation, or hypocrisy."[202]

And these are things you can give, not just for Christmas. You can give them every day of the year.

What Would You Have Done?

In the greatest story ever told, we read about the people who did something to welcome the Christ Child. There were the shepherds on the hills of Bethlehem, watching their flocks by night. There were the wise men who came from afar. And, of course, there were the people of Judea and the scribes and Pharisees—the religious leaders of the day—who were summoned by Herod who asked them where the birth of the Christ Child was going to be?

What if we were in their shoes? Would we have done what they did, or would we have done better? The important thing, however, is that today, we receive Jesus as King and Ruler of our lives.

A poem by Willo Lou Clark brings up this point.

When Chances Come By

If you had been a lowly shepherd who heard the angels sing,
Would you have left your sheep alone to find the baby King?
If you had been the innkeeper—pressed and hurried since the dawn,
Would you have done the best you could, or told them to move on?
If you had been a wise man—due respect and courtly graces,
Would you have left it all behind to search in unknown places?
We cannot know what we'd have done if we had been there then.
We only know what we do now—when chances come again."[203]

Jesus said, "...Inasmuch as you did it to one of the least of these My brethren, you did it to Me" (Matt. 25:40, NKJV).

We will know what we would have done then to the Christ Child by the way in which we treat the least of Christ's brethren today.

All I Want for Christmas

Much of Christmas has always been about giving and receiving. This is so because the birth of Christ—which is the reason for the season—happened as an expression of God's love when He gave His Son to us.

Children especially think about gifts at Christmastime, but more so because they are on the receiving end. In fact, some of them are accustomed to making a list of gifts that they want to receive or have their parents know about it. For adults, much of our time is spent on planning and shopping for gifts we wish to give to family and friends. The gifts we give, however, are those of material value or those that have a dollar sign attached to them.

This Christmas, how about giving something special to your friends and loved ones. How about giving them something that is not measured in dollars and cents but sis so priceless that it goes beyond any material value. I am thinking of the gifts of friendship and other such precious things as love and affection, kindness, care and concern, forgiveness, or even the gift of our time.

Along these lines, I came across a lovely poem that talks about a special gift that we can ask God to give us this Christmas. And this is the gift of prayer—to be able to learn how to pray—not for ourselves, but for our friends and loved ones. To be able to learn how to intercede for others through prayer. This could be the one thing this world is needing, so that the blessings of love, peace, and joy that came upon earth that first Christmas night may become a reality for us today.

The Bible says that God turned the captivity of Job when he prayed and interceded for his friends. He restored Job's losses. In fact, God gave him twice as much as he had before (Job 42:10). And this He did when Job prayed for his friends. And so we can each say this:

"All I want for Christmas is to learn how to pray.
To make this world a better place for friends and family every day.
Jesus, please teach me how to say the words right,
To ensure all are richly blessed on Christmas night.
Please come into my heart and fill it with your love,
So I may always lift them up and send their troubles up above.
Because I know that You, my Savior, my Lord,

Can handle all their cares and wipe away tears that have poured.
Help me, help me, to see Your presence in my soul,
And how focusing on You is what will make them whole.
So please teach me how to pray this Christmas night,
To bring each and every one into Your eternal light."

Would you like to have this gift for Christmas? God is waiting with longing desire to give it to anyone, just as Jesus gave it to His disciples when they came asking Him to teach them to pray.

Merry Christmas everyone and a most prosperous, healthy and happy New Year!

The Christmas Story in Modern Version

The best rendering of the first Christmas event is found in the second chapter of Luke. Here, the gospel evangelist talks about that blessed night when the heavens shone with the glory of an angel who appeared to the shepherds watching their flocks and announced to them the birth of the Savior who is Christ the Lord. And when the shepherds found the baby Jesus lying in a manger, they worshiped and glorified God (Luke 2:8–18).

The Christmas event, however, has been so corrupted and commercialized, and today, when people celebrate Christmas, they think more about stockings, snowmen, Christmas lights, and Christmas trees. In fact, the following is a parody of the words of Luke's narrative; it serves as a sad commentary of what the birth of our Lord means to most people living today.

"And there were in the same country children keeping watch over their presents by the fireplace....

[And the adults were told of] good tidings of great joy which be to all people who can afford them. For unto you will be given great feasts of turkey, dressing, and cake, and many presents; and this shall be a sign unto you, ye shall find the presents, wrapped in bright paper, lying beneath a tree adorned with tinsel, colored balls, and lights.

And suddenly, there will be with you a multitude of relatives and friends, praising you and saying, 'Thank you so much; it was just what I wanted.'

And it shall come to pass as the friends and relatives have gone away into their own homes, the parents shall say to one another, '... What a mess to clean up! I'm tired, let's go to bed and pick it up tomorrow. Thank goodness, Christmas only comes once a year!'

And they go with haste to their bed and find their desired rest."[204]

Is this what you experience when Christmas comes? Then get back to that first Christmas night and let the miracle continue in your heart.

A Time for Sharing

November is Thanksgiving month and December is a time for sharing. No, I'm not referring to the gift-giving and the exchange of gifts that usually happen during the Christmas season. I am talking about sharing our lives, our time, and ourselves—giving that gift to friends and to everyone who may be in need of our friendship.

And the example that God gave us is the best we can follow because, when God gave, He gave His best. When He gave His Son, who is the reason for the season, all heaven was wrapped up in that gift. And if God gave the best, should we give less to Him and to others in need?

Here is inspirational material I want to share with you, as we think of celebrating the season of giving and sharing.

When We Share

> When we share laughter, there's twice the fun;
> When we share success, we surpass what we've done.
> When we share problems, there's half the pain;
> When we share tears, a rainbow follows rain.
> When we share dreams, they become more real;
> When we share secrets, it's our hearts we reveal.
> If we share a smile, then our love shows;
> If we share a hug, then our love grows.
> If we share with someone, on whom we depend,
> That person becomes family or friend.
> And what draws us closer and makes us all care,
> Is not what we have, but the things that we share.[205]

May we all have a season of meaningful giving and joyful sharing.

God Is Like...

"A fifth-grade teacher in a Christian school asked her class to look at TV commercials and see if they could use them in some way to communicate ideas about God. Here are some of the results.

God is like Bayer Aspirin—He works miracles.

God is like a Ford—He's got a better idea.

God is like Coke—He's the real thing.

God is like Hallmark Cards—He cares enough to send His very best.

God is like Tide—He gets the stains out that others leave behind.

God is like General Electric—He brings good things to life.

God is like Sears—He has everything.

God is like Alka-Seltzer—Try Him, you'll like Him.

God is like Scotch Tape—You can't see Him, but you know He's there.

God is like Delta—He's ready when you are.

God is like Allstate—You're in good hands with Him.

God is like VO-5 hair spray—He holds through all kinds of weather.

God is like Dial Soap—Aren't you glad you have Him? Don't you wish everybody did?

God is like the United States Postal Office—Neither rain, nor snow, nor sleet, nor ice will keep Him from His appointed destination.

God is like Maxwell House Coffee—He is good to the very last drop.

God is like Bounty Towels—He is the quicker picker upper. He can handle the tough jogs and He won't fall apart on you.[206]

Jesus has said, "...Out of the mouth of babes and sucklings Thou hast perfected praise!" (Matthew 21:16). And it is so true that we can learn many profound and wonderful things about God and the way He deals with us from the lips of little children.

I just trust that we all can find God to be true in the way He is described here, every moment of every day of our lives.

Special Gifts this Season

Christmas is a happy time of the year. The lights, the trimmings, the carols, the programs, and the parties help make it so. The giving and receiving of gifts also add to the excitement of the holidays. But what do you give to the ones you love, especially when you know they have just about almost everything.

Surfing the internet, I found something I want to share with you. This list is not the usual type of gifts you might plan on giving. But if you think about it, these gifts are ones you can give that would be cherished by your loved ones forever.

"God's Gifts for Family and Friends

1. The gift of LISTENING.

    But you must really listen. No interrupting, no daydreaming, no planning your response.

2. The gift of AFFECTION.

    Be generous with appropriate hugs, kisses, pats on the back, and handholds. Let these small actions demonstrate the love you have for family and friends.

3. The gift of LAUGHTER.

    Share articles and funny stories.

4. The gift of a WRITTEN NOTE.

    A brief, handwritten note may be remembered for a lifetime, and may even change a life.

5. The gift of a COMPLIMENT.

    It can make someone's day.

6. The gift of FAVOR.

   Every day, go out of your way to do something kind.

7. The gift of SOLITUDE.

   There are times when it is important to be left alone. Be sensitive to those moments.

8. The gift of a CHEERFUL DISPOSITION.

   The easiest way to feel good is to extend a kind word to someone."[207]

And I would like to add another gift: THE GIFT OF SALVATION.

It doesn't cost us a cent, but it has been paid for in full by the price of God's own Son, Jesus.

"...The gift of God is eternal Life through Jesus Christ our Lord" (Rom. 6:23).

But, in order to receive this most wonderful of all gifts, you have to accept it through faith. May we receive freely of the gift of salvation offered to us by God. It is priceless—purchased with the blood of Jesus; but it is free when we accept it by faith.

Let us give freely of these gifts. They do not cost us a cent but their value is priceless and they could last a lifetime.

We can start giving these gifts to our friends and loved ones and, as they pick up on it, our gift-giving will be like ripples on a lake that go on in ever-widening circles.

So let the gift-giving begin. And let it continue, not only during the Christmas season, but through every day of the coming years.

The Night Before Christmas

This poem basically tells the story of how Christmas is celebrated or, more accurately, how Christmas is NOT celebrated. It's time we focused our attention on Jesus, the reason for the season, and why God sent His Son to be born among men.

'Twas the month before Christmas and all through the town,
There was not a sign of baby Jesus anywhere to be found;
The people were all busy with their Christmas time chores,
Doing their decorating, baking, and shopping in stores....

When what from their large screen TV did they hear?
But the ad of a big sale going on downtown at Sears;
So away to the mall the family flew like a flash,
Buying things on credit for they had spent all their cash.

They all returned home from their shopping trip at the mall,
Had they thought about Jesus? No, not one of them at all;
Their lives were so busy doing the Christmas time thing,
They had no time to remember Christ Jesus the King.

With so many presents to wrap and all the cookies to bake,
No time was left to remember Jesus Who left it all for their sake;
Instead, it was on Walmart, on K-Mart, on Target, on Penney's,
On Hallmark, on Zales, and catch a quick lunch at Denny's.

There was no room left for the Saviour, no time spent in prayer,
They were too busy for church and lost souls dying in despair;
From the big stores downtown to the small stores at the mall,
It was dash away, dash away, and try to visit them all.

Friend, to the world Christmas is only a holiday season,
But true believers know that Jesus Christ is the real reason;
We must not get so busy that we have no room left for Him,
The One born in a manger Who was not too busy to die for our sins.[208]

So merry Christmas everyone. And may your Christmas be bright because of Christ in Christmas.

As We Celebrate Christmas

Too often, in our celebration of Christmas, we get lost in the festivity of it all. The commercialization of the event has, many a time, buried its real meaning and significance in our lives. However, if we try, I know that this holiday of holidays can still give us the joy that it was meant to bring.

Here's a poem that I hope will help us in our celebration of this event.

Christmas Reminders

"May the Christmas gifts remind you
of God's greatest gift—His only begotten Son.
May the Christmas candles remind you
of Him who is the Light of the World.
May the Christmas tree remind you
of another tree on which He died for you.
May the Christmas cheer remind
of Him who said, 'Be of good cheer.'"[209]
May the Christmas feast remind you
of Him who is the Bread of Life.
May the Christmas snow remind you
of the cleansing power of Christ.
"May the Christmas bells remind you
of the glorious proclamation of His birth.
May the Christmas carols remind you
of His glad tidings which we are to proclaim.
May the Christmas season remind you
in every way of Jesus Christ, your king."[210]

Why Jesus is the Reason for the Season

As we join the rest of the Christian world in celebrating the birth of Jesus, let us make sure that we do not lose sight of the reason Jesus left the glories of heaven to come down to earth and be born as a little child and ultimately offer His life to the world. True, we have glamorized the manger and have romanticized and commercialized the virgin birth.

The parties, the decorations and the lights, the shopping and the gift-giving are all symbolic and are a celebratory result of the supreme gift of heaven to the human family.

But let not the gift itself be outclassed by the packaging and the wraps. Let us not lose sight of the true meaning of God's gift to us, His undeserving children.

The following material will help us focus on why Jesus came, and I trust that our Christmas celebrations now, and in the years ahead, will become much more meaningful with these thoughts.

Why Jesus?

JESUS was born, that I might be born twice.
HE became poor, that I might possess wealth.
HE became homeless, that I might have a mansion.
HE was stripped, that I always should have clothes.
HE was forsaken, that I always should have friends.
HE was bound, that I might have perfect liberty.
HE was sad, that I might have full joy.
HE descended, that I should be lifted up.
HE became a servant, that I might be a son forever.
He was hungry, that I should always have food.
HE was made sin, that I should share His righteousness.
HE died, that I should never taste eternal death.
HE will come down, that I might go up.
All of this- that He might display in me the riches of His grace,
And be the companion of God in the heavenlies."[211]

What Kind of Church Are We?

A church is a group of people called out by God to tell the world of His love and His wonderful plan of redemption. It is not a club or a group of people organized merely for social functions or activities. Some churches admirably live up to their mission. Others deteriorate until they lose sight of their goals and simply die. The material below shows the difference between a church that is alive and one that is dead.

A Lively Church

A lively church has parking problems;

A dead church doesn't.

A lively church has lots of 'noisy' children and young people;

A dead church is fairly quiet.

A lively church often changes the way things are done;

A dead church doesn't.

A lively church often asks for more program and mission money;

A dead church tries to keep plenty of money in the treasury.

A lively church asks people to open up and risk involvement;

A dead church plays it safe and never risks.

A lively church sees challenges and opportunities;

A dead church sees problems and dangers.

A lively church apologizes, forgives, and seeks forgiveness;

A dead church never makes mistakes.

A lively church uses its tradition and facilities to serve people;

A dead church uses people to preserve facilities and traditions.

A lively church believes in God's future and 'let's go' with faith;

A dead church believes in the past and 'holds on.'

A lively church is filled with committed givers;

A dead church is filled with tippers.

A lively church dares to dream great dreams for God's kingdom;

A dead church has nightmares."[212]

So, are we more of a lively church or more of a dead church. Whatever the answer, we can decide to be a lively church and stay that way.

Marks of Revival

Israel was mainly an agricultural economy, and the Bible writers who lived in this setting made use of the things that the people were familiar with to illustrate the eternal things of the kingdom. One thing that was important then was the rain that was so necessary for the crops to grow and mature.

Rain is still a crucial need in the Middle East to this day, but it was a more critical need then. There was a former or early rain that came in the spring that made the crops grow and mature during the planting season. And then came the latter rain in the fall that was so necessary for the crops to ripen for the harvest.

In Hosea 6:3, we find these words: "Then shall we know, if we follow on to know the Lord: his going forth is prepared as the morning; and he shall come unto us as the rain, as the latter and former rain unto the earth."

In this passage of Scripture, we are given a glimpse of how God does His work of making us grow and ripen for His harvest. The Holy Spirit comes to us and generates spiritual life in our lifeless souls. Then, even as He continues to sustain us in our everyday life in the spirit, He promises to come upon us as the latter rain that will make us spiritually ready for glorification into His kingdom.

The latter rain experience in the spiritual life is sometimes called a *revival*, and this comes as the result of earnest prayer and daily seeking of His Word. As the soul is engaged in these activities, the much-needed and prayed-for revival will happen.

How do we know that this is happening in our lives? Three things.

1. We will seek to make our hearts right with God every moment through private devotions and prayer.

2. We will enjoy the fellowship of Bible study and prayer and will want to pray together in small groups and little bands.

3. We will want to allow God to use us as an instrument in seeking the lost and bringing them back to His fold.

So may these be the hallmarks of our Christian experience as we live for God each day and as we await and prepare for Christ's soon return.

Communion—A Time for Rededication

It's amazing how days of neglect of our spiritual lives can take us away from God and make it difficult to re-establish that connection once again. That's why Ellen White says we need to consecrate ourselves to God every morning and making this our first task.[213] But Communion is a special time, and, as we come before the Lord's table, we have the privilege of renewing our vows of loyalty to Him as Lord and Savior of our lives.

The following poem expresses this beautiful thought.

I looked upon a farm one day,
that once I used to own;
The barn had fallen to the ground,
the fields were overgrown.
It was the house of my youth,
where we had lived for years
And as I viewed it all broken down,
I brushed aside the tears.

I looked upon my soul one day, it too was overgrown,
with thorns and weeds of neglect, all seeds that I had sown.
Many years had passed
while I had cared for things of lesser worth.
The things of heaven I had let go
To mind the things of earth.

And weeping with bitter tears, I cried,
"Oh Lord, please forgive!"
I have not much time left for Thee,
not many years to live.
Those wasted years are forever gone,
They're days I can't recall.
If I could live those days again,
I'd make You Lord of all.[214]

Are You Faithful?

How would you stand if you applied the same standards of faithfulness to your Christian activities that you apply to other areas of your life? Are you going to pass as faithful and dependable?

"If your car starts once every three tries, is it reliable?

If your postman skips delivery every Monday and Thursday, is he trustworthy?

If you don't go to work once or twice a month, are you a reliable employee?

If your refrigerator stops working for a day or two every now and then, do you say, 'Oh, well, it works most of the time'?

If you fail to worship God one or two [Sabbaths] a month, would you expect to be called a faithful Christian?"[215]

We expect faithfulness and reliability from people and things. Does not God expect the same from us?

The problem is that, in our religious activities, we see ourselves as volunteers rather than as duty bound (1 Cor. 9). For a volunteer, almost anything seems acceptable. For a bondservant who is duty bound, faithfulness is expected (Matt. 25:21).

So, back to the question: Are you faithful?

And yes, I mean YOU!

Lose Weight by Turning the TV Off

This is not a joke. Researchers say that TV is "fattening.". By simply turning the TV off, you reduce your risk of becoming or being overweight. And, in addition, it could improve your general health, help you communicate more with your family and friends, and save you money too!

Studies of the viewing habits of Americans by Dr. Larry Tucker and his colleagues at Brigham Young University showed that your chances for unhealthy obesity (defined as 30% or more of body fat) more than doubled when viewers spent 3 or 4 hours in front of the TV.[216] Unfortunately, many people spend about that much time each day watching TV.

Now I am not saying you should throw your TV out the window. I suggest that you should limit its negative impact on your physical, mental, and spiritual health.

Here are a few suggestions:

1. Have a TV program guide and schedule your viewing time each week. After choosing the programs you want to watch, stick to your schedule. Stop switching from channel to channel. Turn off the TV when the program is over.

2. When not doing anything, get out of the house. Take a walk. Do some gardening or visit with your neighbors.

3. When the TV is off and you can't get out of the house, find some devotional book and read or write some letters to friends. Think of some improvement you can make in the house. You'll be surprised at how many creative ideas you can come up with during this "TV off" time.

And remember a nice TV guideline from the scripture:
"Whatsoever things are true, whatsoever things are honest, whatsoever things are just, whatsoever things are pure, whatsoever things are lovely, whatsoever things are of good report; if there be any virtue and if there be any praise, think on these things" (Phil. 4:8).

Just Suppose

As we come close to the end of time, we will find it more and more difficult to maintain a vibrant faith in the Lord and to be an aggressive witness for the advancement of His Kingdom. The allurements of the world and the bewitching influence of the finer things of this life are inflicting a stupefying effect upon the soul, and not a few professed Christians suffer from this deathly spiritual stupor that comes as a natural result.

This ought not to surprise us. Laodicea, the seventh and final church of Revelation, is characterized as being lukewarm. in its spirituality and being nauseous to the taste (Rev. 3:16).

And Jesus Himself said, "...When the Son of man cometh, shall He find faith on the earth?" (Luke 18:8).

Now, I just thought that we should take a little time to do a spiritual check on ourselves, on how we measure up to our professed beliefs and commitments. I came across a set of questions that I thought would be good for us to ask ourselves and compare our answers to our Christian life and performance.

How about going through these questions at this time.

"Suppose you had to run for church membership as a candidate runs for a political office. Would you win or lose?

Suppose your membership was good for only one year and that your reelection depended upon the good you had done in the church during that time? Would you be reelected?

Suppose your name would be dropped from membership if you didn't win to Christ at least one person a year. How long would you remain a member?

Suppose you were asked to explain just why your church should keep your name on the roll. Do you have a record of helpful service to offer in your defense?

Suppose every member in the church did as much work for the church as you are presently doing. Would more seats be needed, or would the doors of the church be closed.

Suppose you were arrested for being a Christian. Would there be enough evidence to convict you?"[217]

It Has Been a Good Year, Thank God

As the final days of the year trickle down through the hourglass of time, we look back and ponder how the year has been. And as we look back at the year, from beginning to end, we see how God has been so good to us.

It was a tough year for many of us, but the Lord blessed and sustained us all, and here we are at the end of the year, proclaiming His goodness and looking forward to the dawning of another year.

While we do not know what awaits us in the New Year, we can be confident that He who preserved our comings and goings this past year will do the same for us in the days ahead. For has He not declared that He is "… the same yesterday, and today, and forever"? (Heb. 13:8).

Let us therefore look forward with hope and courage to the coming year. For though we may be beset with trials, sorrow, or pain and though uncertainties lurk at every turn, He who holds us with His hands will not let us go for as long as we continue to hold onto Him.

Wishing you all a blessed New Year!

Resolutions for the New Year

Jonathan Edwards was, to some, the greatest American preacher, philosopher, and theologian who lived in the early 18th century. In volume 1 of his works, he writes about his resolutions, which are well worth our time and effort to read and model after, especially as we think of living a life that is pleasing in the sight of God.

How about picking a few, or even all, of these resolutions and making them our own, resolving, by God's grace, to live by them this New Year and throughout the remaining days of our lives?

"1. Resolved, that I will do whatsoever I think to be most to the glory of God...

2. Resolved, to do whatever I think to be my duty, and most for the good and advantage of mankind in general.

3. Resolved, Never to lose one moment of time, but to improve it in the most profitable way I possibly can.

4. Resolved, To live with all my might, while I do live.

5. Resolved, Never to do anything, which I should be afraid to do if it were the last hour of my life.

6. Resolved, Never to do anything out of revenge.

7. Resolved, Never to speak evil of any one, so that it shall tend to his dishonor, more or less, upon no account except for some real good.

8. Resolved, To study the Scriptures so steadily, constantly, and frequently, as that I may find, and plainly perceive, myself to grow in the knowledge of the same.

9. Resolved, Never to count that a prayer, nor to let that pass as a prayer, nor that as a petition of a prayer, which is so made, that I cannot hope that God will answer it; nor that as a confession which I cannot hope God will accept.

10. Resolved, To ask myself, at the end of every day, week, month, and year, wherein I could possibly, in any respect, have done better.

11. Resolved, Never to give over, nor in the least to slacken, my fight with my corruptions, however unsuccessful I may be.

12. Resolved, After afflictions, to inquire, what I am the better for them; what good I have got by them, and what I might have got by them.

13. Resolved, Always to do that which I shall wish I had done when I see others do it.

14. Let there be something of benevolence in all that I speak.[218]

A Happy New Year to everyone and may your living be rewarding, impactful, and satisfying as we resolve to live our best for Him.

New Year's Resolutions

The New Year is a time to look back and see how we did in the past year. It is a time to make adjustments and changes in our habits and our lifestyle, so that we can avoid the mistakes we made and achieve our human potential in the days ahead.

One of the things we can do to make this happen is to make resolutions for the New Year so that the coming year will be a better one.

The following are suggestions I have for all of us, so that this year can be a good one, if not the best ever in our lives.

1. Have a closer walk with God. Putting first things first makes everything fall into place.

2. Spend more time with family and friends. When life comes down to its very end, it's family and friends that we long for. It's relationships that are important. Houses, cars, money and material things count for nothing in the final analysis.

3. Take good care of your health. This is the only way you can enjoy life and be able to achieve your maximum potential.

4. Enjoy life more. It's too precious and too short and so uncertain. Have fun while you can.

5. Be more helpful to others. Happiness comes when you turn away from self and focus on others.

6. Get involved in a charity project. You'll feel better when you know you are making a difference in the life of another.

7. Be more organized. Life flows more smoothly when it is well organized. You don't even have to work so hard. Just working smarter will do the trick.

8. Get out of debt. It is still true, "...the borrower is the slave of the lender" (Prov. 22:7, ESV). Freedom is still a sweet and precious thing to have.

9. Learn something new. There is a world of fun and excitement out there. Don't miss out on what you can enjoy that is right at your fingertips.

10. Reward yourself for following through with these resolutions throughout the year and the rest of your life. Don't make it hard on yourself. You need that boost.

Here's wishing you the best for the coming year.

About the Author

Simeon Rosete was born in the Philippines and earned a degree in the History and Philosophy of Religion at Philippine Union College, now Adventist University of the Philippines. He went on to complete his Master's degree in Theology and Public Health at the Seventh-day Adventist Theological Seminary (Far East) in Manila, Philippines. He would later earn the degree of Doctor of Biblical Studies at the Master's International School of Divinity in Evansville, Indiana.

He has served as a pastor, department director, and finally president of the Mountain Provinces Mission of Seventh-day Adventists, with headquarters at Baguio City, Philippines. He was elected president at the age of 28, making him the youngest Mission president in the history of the work of the Seventh-day Adventist Church in the Philippines.

He was called to serve as the senior pastor of the Central Filipino Seventh-day Adventist Church in Los Angeles, California, a 600-member congregation, and the first Filipino Seventh-day Adventist Church established in the United States and Canada. He has served this congregation for 25 years now and was instrumental in the construction of its sanctuary and gymnasium complex.

In between his ministry to the Central Filipino Church, he served as director of the Asian Pacific Region of the Southern California Conference of Seventh-day Adventists, with headquarters at Glendale, California, and also served as senior pastor of the Glendale Filipino Seventh-day Adventist Church, Glendale, California.

He is married to the former Ellen Pacheco, with whom he has four children; they also have four grandchildren.

Endnotes

1. Levenson, Sam. *In One Era and Out the Other.* New York, NY: Pocket Books (Simon & Schuster), 1973.
2. "Audrey Hepburn > Quotes > Quotable Quote." Goodreads, Inc. 2019. Accessed July 23, 2019, https://1ref.us/z6.
3. "Audrey Hepburn > Quotes > Quotable Quote." Goodreads, Inc. 2019. Accessed July 23, 2019, https://1ref.us/z7.
4. "Audrey Hepburn > Quotes > Quotable Quote." Goodreads, Inc. 2019. Accessed July 23, 2019, https://1ref.us/z8.
5. "Another Year Is Dawning." Hymntime, 1996–2019. Accessed July 23, 2019, https://1ref.us/zh.
6. White, Ellen G. *Selected Messages.* Book 1., Washington, DC: Review and Herald Publishing Association, 1958, p. 121.
7. Morgan, G. Campbell. "Christian Quotes: 59 Quotes About Revival." 2019. Accessed July 24, 2019, https://1ref.us/zi.
8. Coleman, Robert E. *The Heart of the Gospel: The Theology behind the Master Plan of Evangelism.* Ada, MI: BakerBooks (Baker Publishing Group), 2011, p. 225.
9. "The Eagle." AllWorship. Accessed July 24, 2019, https://1ref.us/zj.
10. Pattison, John Erik. "Side by Side: The Parable of the Two Brothers." 2019. Accessed July 24, 2019, https://1ref.us/zk.
11. Cade, Chris. "The Obstacles in Our Path." Spiritual Short Stories. Parables. Accessed July 24, 2019, https://1ref.us/zl.
12. Jeremiah, David. "A Risen King!" *Sanctuary: Finding Moments of Refuge in the Presence of God.* Accessed July 24, 2019. Nashville, TN: Thomas Nelson, Inc., 2002.
13. St. John Cantius Church. "The Feast of the Epiphany of the Lord." Jan. 2, 2001. Accessed July 24, 2019, https://1ref.us/zm.
14. Keys, Jerrilene. "The Secret." *Unforgettables? "Inspirational" Quotes, Sayings & Readings.* Maitland, FL: Xulon Press, 2010, pp. 110–111.

15   Wikipedia. "Bed of roses." 2019. Accessed October 21, 2019, https://1ref.us/zn.
16   Patterson, Steve. "Courageous Christian Father." 2012—2019. Accessed October 21, 2019, https://1ref.us/zo.
17   Welsh, Destiny. "The Joyful Things." The Well: An Encounter for Women. 2017. Accessed July 26, 2019, https://1ref.us/zp.
18   Taylor, Ida S., ed. "January Thirty-First," by Proctor, Adelaide. *Year Book of English Authors*. New York, NY: H. M. Caldwell Co., 1894, p. 37.
19   Dyer, William. "The Desire of All Nations." *Christ's Famous Titles*. London: Milner and Sowerby, Paternoster Row, 1865, p. 16.
20   Charles Schultz Philosophy. 1997. Accessed July 27, 2019, https://1ref.us/zq.
21   Ibid.
22   Theodore Roosevelt. Accessed July 27, 2019, https://1ref.us/zr.
23   Charles Schultz Philosophy. 1997. Accessed July 27, 2019, https://1ref.us/zq.
24   Theodore Roosevelt. Accessed July 27, 2019, https://1ref.us/zr.
25   Popkin, Roy. "Night Watch." *Reader's Digest*, September 1964. New York, NY: Simon & Schuster.
26   Stamm, Millie. "January 2." *Be Still and Know*. Grand Rapids, MI: Zondervan Publishing House, 1978.
27   Preaching Today.com, eds. "Judging Others." *More Perfect Illustrations for Every Topic and Occasion*. Wheaton, IL: Tyndale Publishers, Inc., 2003, p. 153.
28   Quoteland.com. "American Indian Proverb." 1997–2001. Accessed July 28, 2019, https://1ref.us/zs.
29   M Stories. "Rose for Mother." 2019. Accessed July 29, 2019, https://1ref.us/zt.
30   Rice, Wayne. "Awesome Obedience." *Hot Illustrations for Youth Talks: 100 Attention-Getting Stories*. Grand Rapids, MI: Zondervan Publishing, 1994.
31   Ari Schonbrun. "A Woman & a Fork." 2017. Accessed July 28, 2019, https://1ref.us/zu.

32. Victor Hafichuk. "The Brick." The Path of Truth. 2019. Accessed July 28, 2019, https://1ref.us/zv.

33. Eggleston. Jane. "It's in the Valleys I Grow." Accessed July 28, 2019, https://1ref.us/zw.

34. Harris, Gerald. "The Divine Mandate." Pastor Life. 2019. Accessed July 28, 2019, https://1ref.us/zx.

35. Lyubomirsky, Sonja. *The How of Happiness: A Scientific Approach to Getting the Life You Want*. New York, NY: The Penguin Press, 2008.

36. Wolfe, Moshe. "Chaplain's Corner: Take a Moment to Ponder." *Chicago FOP Lodge #7 Newsletter*. 2004, p. 6. Accessed July 28, 2019, https://1ref.us/zy.

37. Swindoll, Charles R. "Salvation." *The Tale of the Tardy Oxcart*. Nashville, TN: Thomas Nelson, 1998. Accessed July 28, 2019, https://1ref.us/zz.

38. Daniel, Thomas. "36 Christian Ways to Reduce Stress." Holistic Living: A Place to Relax. 1998–2013 ICBS. Accessed August 5, 2019, https://1ref.us/100.

39. Wikipedia. "Know thyself." July 13, 2019. Accessed August 6, 2019, https://1ref.us/101.

40. Tozer, Aiden W. *That Incredible Christian: How Heaven's Children Live on Earth*. Carol Stream, IL: Tyndale House Publishers, 1964.

41. Batterson, Mark. *The Circle Maker: Praying Circles Around Your Biggest Dreams and Greatest Fears*. Grand Rapids, MI: Zondervan, 2016.

42. Backholer, Mathew. *Extreme Faith, On Fire Christianity: Hearing from God and Moving in His Grace, Strength & Power, Living in Victory*. 2013, 2014, 2015, 2016, 2017. ByFaith Media. Accessed February 12, 2020, https://1ref.us/102.

43. White, Ellen G. *Christ's Object Lessons*. Washington, DC: Review and Herald Publishing Association, 1900, p. 331.1.

44. Hadley, R. F. "The Tater People." 2002. Accessed August 6, 2019, https://1ref.us/103.

45. "William Cowper > Quotes > Quotable Quote 1785." Goodreads, Inc. 2019. Accessed August 8, 2019, https://1ref.us/104.

46 Waitley, Denis. *Seeds of Greatness: The Ten Best-Kept Secrets of Total Success*. New York, NY: Gallery Books (Simon & Schuster), 2010.

47 "Mahatma Gandhi > Quotes > Quotable Quote." Goodreads, Inc. 2019. Accessed August 6, 2019, https://1ref.us/105.

48 Osbeck, Kenneth W. *101 Hymn Stories: The Inspiring True Stories Behind 101 Favorite Hymns*. Grand Rapids, MI: Kregel Publications, 1982.

49 Ibid.

50 Caron, Michael. "The Weekly Spotlight of Friends." 2006. Accessed August 6, 2019, https://1ref.us/106.

51 Hamlin, Rick. "Five Classic Christian Prayers: Prayer of a Confederate Soldier." *Guideposts*, 2010. Accessed August 6, 2019, https://1ref.us/107.

52 "God's Hand." *Eastern Canadian Messenger*, vol. 26, issue 28, July 20, 1926, p. 8. Accessed August 6, 2019, https://1ref.us/108.

53 Moore, David William. "A Little Poem." FindMyWings. January 23, 2009. Accessed August 7 2019, https://1ref.us/109.

54 Frankel, Ellen. "109, This Too Shall Pass." *The Classic Tales: 4,000 Years of Jewish Lore*. Lanham, MD: Jason Aronson, Inc., 1993, pp. 257–260.

55 Martin-Del-Campo, Frederick. *A Wetback in Reverse: Hunting for an American in the Wilds of Mexico*. British Columbia, Canada: CCB Publishing, 2013, pp. 52–54.

56 "I Believe, …." KindSpring: Small Acts That Change The World. 2018. Accessed August 7, 2019, https://1ref.us/10a.

57 "Words of wisdom: I've learned that…" 1997. Accessed August 7, 2019, https://1ref.us/10b.

58 "I Believe…." KindSpring: Small Acts That Change The World. 2018. Accessed August 7, 2019, https://1ref.us/10a.

59 "18 Proven Stress Reducers." Bible.org. 2019. Accessed August 7, 2019, https://1ref.us/10c.

60 "The Ship of Friendship." M Stories. 2019. Accessed August 7, 2019, https://1ref.us/10d.

61 Nixon, David J. "The Best Poem in the World." 1996. Accessed August 8, 2019, https://1ref.us/10e.

62 Keller, Helen. *We Bereaved*. New York, NY: Leslie Fulenwider Publisher, 1929. "Helen Keller Quotes on Happiness." 2019. Accessed August 8, 2019, https://1ref.us/10f.

63 "Henry of Bavaria." StoriesforPreaching.com. 2019. From *Leadership* Vol. 6 (Fall 1985).

64 Brown, Paul B. "'You Miss 100% of the Shots You Don't Take.' You Need to Start Shooting at Your Goals." *Forbes*. 2014. Accessed August 8, 2019, https://1ref.us/10q.

65 "John C. Maxwell > Quotes >Quotable Quote." Goodreads, Inc. 2019. Accessed August 8, 2019, https://1ref.us/10r.

66 Burkett, Larry. Business by the Book: *The Complete Guide of Biblical Principles for the Workplace*. Nashville, TN: Thomas Nelson, Inc., 1998.

67 Adams, David V. *Lifestyle Worship: The Worship God Intended Then and Now*. Eugene, OR: Resource Publications, 2010, p. 115.

68 White, Ellen G. *The Great Controversy*. Mountain View, CA: Pacific Press Publishing Association, 1911, p. 593.2.

69 Fessenden, Marissa. "There Are Now More American Over Age 100 and They're Living Longer than Ever." 2016. Accessed August 8, 2019, https://1ref.us/10s.

70 Jung, Alyssa, and Jones, Meghan. "15 Science-Backed Signs You Could Live to Be 100." *Reader's Digest*, July/August 2018.

71 Nooruddin, Mustafa. "Burden of Life." *Morals of Life Stories*. Chetpet, Chennai: Notion Press, 2018.

72 Ward, William Arthur. "Risk." Inspirational Words of Wisdom. Accessed August 8, 2019, https://1ref.us/10t.

73 Churnin, Nancy, and Popovici, Danny. *Manjhi Moves a Mountain*. Berkeley, CA: Creston Books, 2017.

74 Rader, Paul. "Let Go and Let God." 2007–present. Accessed August 8, 2019, https://1ref.us/10u.

75 "The Touch of the Master's Hand." "Myra Brooks Welch > Quotes > Quotable Quote." Goodreads, Inc. 2019. Accessed August 8, 2019, https://1ref.us/10v.

76 "The Story of the Woodcutter"—by Stephen Covey from *The 7 Habits of Highly Effective People.*" 2013. Accessed August 8, 2019, https://1ref.us/10w.

77 White, Ellen G. *Steps to Christ*. Mountain View, CA: Pacific Press Publishing Association, 1892, 70.1.

78 "5 Signs It's Time to Change Your Life." Motivation Seeds. 2019. Accessed August 10, 2019, https://1ref.us/10x.

79 White, Ellen G. *Patriarchs and Prophets*. Washington, DC: Review and Herald Publishing Association, 1890, pp. 44, 49.

80 Hewitt, James S. *Illustrations Unlimited*. Carol Stream, IL: Tyndale House Publishers, Inc., 1988, p. 91.

81 McNerny, Samuel. "A Brief Guide to Embodied Cognition: Why You Are Not Your Brain." *Scientific American*. 2011. Accessed August 10, 2019, https://1ref.us/10y.

82 Rosete, Simeon P., Jr. "How Much Stuff Do We Really Need?" *Inspiring Thoughts to Jump Start Your Day*. Staten Island, NY: Page Publishing Inc., 2019.

83 Lake, Rebecca. "Grocery Shopping Statistics: 23 Fun Size Facts to Know." CreditDonkey. Accessed August 10, 2019, https://1ref.us/10z.

84 Kahn, Joel K., MD, "The 6 Most Dangerous Times for Your Heart, According to a Cardiologist." *Reader's Digest* 2018-03-28. Accessed February 17, 2020, https://1ref.us/110.

85 "World of Medicine: High-Fat Diet Hurts Sleep." *Reader's Digest Asia*. 2017-03-01.

86 "Executive Summary: Dietary Guidelines 2015–2020." Office of Disease Prevention and Health Promotion. Accessed, August 21, 2019, https://1ref.us/112.

87 Small, Gary, MD. *The Alzheimer's Prevention Program: Keep Your Brain Healthy for the Rest of Your Life.* New York, NY: Workman Publishing Company, 2012.

88 "Science News: The Less Older Adults Sleep, the Faster Their Brains Age, New Study Suggests." ScienceDaily July 1, 2014. Accessed August 22, 2019, https://1ref.us/111.

89 "Brain May Flush Out Toxins During Sleep." National Institutes of Health. October 17, 2013. Accessed August 22, 2019. https://1ref.us/113.

90 "Science News: Grandmas Stay Sharp When They Care for Grandkids Once a Week" ScienceDaily. April 8, 2014. Accessed August 22, 2019, https://1ref.us/114.

91 Rothman, Lilly. "How Woodstock Led to National Grandparents Day." *Time*. August 3, 1970. Accessed August 22, 2019, https://1ref.us/115.

92 Rourke, Mary. "Advocate for Elderly Founded Grandparents Day." *Los Angeles Times*. October 2, 2008. Accessed August 22, 2019, https://1ref.us/116.

93 "Eric Hoffer > Quotes > Quotable Quote. Goodreads, Inc. 2019. Accessed August 22, 2019, https://1ref.us/117.

94 "Still Munching Candy." From *Parade Magazine* February 11, 1962. 2009. Bible.org. 2019. Accessed August 22, 2019, https://1ref.us/118.

95 "If You Want to Kill the Church." Bible.org. 2019. Accessed August 22, 2019, https://1ref.us/119.

96 "Long Ago, There Ruled in Persia a Wise and Good…" SermonCentral, 2003–2019. Accessed August 22, 2019, https://1ref.us/11a.

97 White, Ellen G. *Fundamentals of Christian Education*. Nashville, TN: Southern Publishing Association, 1923, p. 214.1.

98 Johnson, Moses, Sr., and Johnson, Vivian M. *Daily Inspiration Thru God's Word*. Bloomington, IN: WestBow Press Publishing, 2014, p. 7.

99 "My Mother." Bible.org, 2019. Accessed August 22, 2019, https://1ref.us/11b.

100 "David Livingston: Missionary (1813–1873)." Biography.com, 2019. Accessed August 22, 2019, https://1ref.us/11c.

101 "A Good Road." April 1985 Good News Broadcast, p. 12. Sermonsearch. Accessed August 22, 2019, https://1ref.us/11d.

102 Wong, Mike. "God Never Makes Mistakes." Central Filipino Seventh-Day Adventist Church. 2018. Accessed August 22, 2019, https://1ref.us/11e.

103 "Charles Haddon Spurgeon > Quotes > Quotable Quote." Goodreads, Inc. 2019. Accessed August 23, 2019, https://1ref.us/11f.

104 Chalakoski, Marin. "Bobby Leach, first man to survive Niagara Falls barrel plunge, died after slipping on orange peel." *The Vintage News*. July 6, 2017. Accessed August 23, 2019, https://1ref.us/11g.

105 "A Good President." Bible.org. February 4, 1993. Accessed August 23, 2019, https://1ref.us/11h.

106 Zhao, Christina. "Las Vegas Shooter Stephen Paddock Kept Staring at Mandalay Bay Housekeeper. *Newsweek*. <au 17. 2018. Accessed August 23, 2019, https://1ref.us/11i.

107 King, Esther B. *Think on These Things*. Bloomington, IN: Xlibris Corporation, 2011, p. 166.

108 "Misery Dinner." Christopher News Notes, August 1993. Bible.org. Accessed August 23, 2019, https://1ref.us/11j.

109 Miller, Dan. "Perspective: Tragedy or Blessing?" *48 Days to the Work You Love*. Nashville, TN: B&H Publishing Group, 2007, p. 25.

110 Carlyle, Thomas. "If Only I Had Known." January 10, 2017. Accessed February 17, 2020, https://1ref.us/11k.

111 Keating, Ronan. "If Tomorrow Never Comes." LyricFind. Accessed February 17, 2020, https://1ref.us/11l.

112 "Introduction: Gregory Elder Tells of Growing Up." SermonCentral. 2003–2019. Accessed August 25, 2019, https://1ref.us/11m.

113 "#612 Onward, Christian Soldiers." *SDA Hymnal*. February 2, 2009. Accessed August 25, 2019, https://1ref.us/11n.

114 "Backward Christian Soldiers." Bible.org. 2019. Accessed August 25, 2019, https://1ref.us/11o.

115 "The Da Vinci Code (film)." Wikipedia, 2019. Accessed August 25, 2019, https://1ref.us/11p.

116 Mehaffie, Sam. *Every Man's a Mentor*. Maitland, FL: Xulon Press, 2005, p. 63.

117 "Cell Phone vs. Bible." SermonIndex.net, November 11, 2004. Accessed August 25, 2019, https://1ref.us/11q.

118 "The Lord Is My Shepherd." Cobblestone Road Ministries, 2012. Accessed August 26, 2019, https://1ref.us/11r.

119 "Signs of Spiritual Awakening." December 6, 2013. Accessed August 25, 2019, https://1ref.us/11s.

120 Author unknown.

121 Tiang, April. *Age Does not Define Me: I Do!* Bloomington, IN: Xlibris Corporation, 2012, p. 95.

122 "Life Can Begin at 40/50/60/70, It Is All in Your Hands." Enjoying Wonderful World, October 17, 2011. Accessed August 26, 2019, https://1ref.us/11t.

123 Hoaglund, Maria Dancing Heart. *The Last Adventure in Life: Sacred Resources for Living and Dying from a Hospice Counselor.* Sidney, Australia: Finch Publishing, 2009, p. 67.

124 Purdum, Stan, and Thompson, Gary. "Monday, March 11, Ephesians 2:1–10, Transformed by Christ into New Life." *Daily Bible Study Spring 2019*. Nashville, TN: Cokesbury/United Methodist Publishing House, 2019.

125 "John Wesley > Quotes > Quotable Quote." Goodreads, Inc. 2019. Accessed August 26, 2019, https://1ref.us/11u.

126 Dykstra, Ron. "Good Stuff." *Clean Jokes, Inspirational Stories and More*. Mustang: OK: Tate Publishing Enterprises, 2009, p. 212.

127 Allaway, Al, ed. "Christian One-Liners." *E-Praise 4 Gifting: Christian E-Mail Devotions*. Al & Del Allaway publishing, 2008, p. 47.

128 "Augustine of Hippo > Quotes > Quotable Quote." Goodreads, Inc. 2019. Accessed August 26, 2019, https://1ref.us/11v.

129 "Lyman Bryson > Quotes." Goodreads, Inc. 2019. Accessed August 26, 2019, https://1ref.us/11w.

130 Stiles, Mark. "Things I Wish I Would Have Known Before I Was Twenty-One." *Mentoring Youth in Action: Seven Lessons to Increase the Significance of Christianity in Our Youth*. Bloomington, IN: iUniverse, Inc., pp. 62–63.

131 Rowell, Edward K. "Finishing Well." *1001 Quotes, Illustrations, and Humorous Stories for Preachers, Teachers, and Writers*. Grand Rapids, MI: Baker Books, 2008, p. 258.

132 *Faith in Action*, p. 1. September 2011. Accessed August 26, 2019, https://1ref.us/11x.

133 Thompson, Roger. *Horsin' Around.* September 10, 2007. Accessed August 26, 2019, https://1ref.us/11y.

134 Morrow, Quinton. "Finders, Keepers." July 9, 2002. Accessed August 26, 2019, https://1ref.us/11z.

135 "Being a Christian Is Like Being a Pumpkin." Inspirational Christian Stories and Poems. May 22, 2011. Accessed August 27, 2019, https://1ref.us/120.

136 Coon, Carlton, Sr. Discipleship. May 20, 2019. From *Preaching* magazine. Accessed October 22, 2019, https://1ref.us/121.

137 Lomax, Stephen S. *What You Don't Know Can Not Only Hurt You, But Destroy You.* Bloomington, IN: AuthorHouse, 2009, p. 235.

138 Hewett, James S., ed. "Prescription for Unhappiness." *Illustrations Unlimited*. Wheaton, IL: Tyndale House Publishers, Inc., p. 281.

139 "How to Be Perfectly Miserable." *Gospel Herald*. Aspire Higher Motivational Quotes. Accessed August 26, 2019, https://1ref.us/122.

140 Ross, Sharilyn A. "Eight Special Qualities of the Spiritually Mature." *The Spirit of Camp*. Maitland, FL: Xulon Press, 2010, p. 201.

141 Miller, Cheryl. "Life Lessons from a Butterfly." *Healthy Habits: 21 Day Challenge*. CherylMillerVille, 2007, p. 2.

142 "Benjamin Franklin > Quotes > Quotable Quote." Goodreads, Inc. 2019. Accessed August 27, 2019, https://1ref.us/123.

143 "Where God Ain't." Cobblestone Road Ministries, 2006. Accessed August 27, 2019, https://1ref.us/124.

144 Hewett, James S., ed. "How Does Your Church Score?" *Illustrations Unlimited*. Wheaton, IL: Tyndale House Publishers, Inc., 1988, pp. 94–95.

145 "Serenity Prayer Words." Bibleinfo, 2019. Accessed August 27, 2019, https://1ref.us/125.

146 "ACA Serenity Prayer." Adult Children of Alcoholics World Service Organization. 2018. Accessed August 27, 2019, https://1ref.us/126.

147 Bachelor, Doug. *The Book of Amazing Facts*. Roseville, CA: Amazing Facts, Incorporated, 2002, p. 12.

148 Thompson, John L. *Urban Impact: Reaching the World through Effective Urban Ministry*. Eugene, OR: Wipf & Stock Publishers, 2010, p. 32.

149 Donne, John. *No Man Is an Island*. London: Souvenir Press, 1988.

150 "The Mountain Climber." Heaven Awaits. Accessed August 27, 2019, https://1ref.us/127.

151 Payne, Robert. *From the Heart: Stories of Hope, Passion, and Purpose*. Gretna, LA: Pelican Publishing Company, Inc., 2012, p. 182.

152 Haney, T. Ronald. *Advent and Christian Meditations*. Bloomington, IN: AuthorHouse, 2007, pp. 2–3.

153 Bond, Michael. New Scientist. "The Pursuit of Happiness." October 4, 2003. Accessed August 27, 2019, https://1ref.us/128.

154 Ibid.

155 Wikipedia. "Mercer Quality of Living Survey." August 17, 2019. Accessed August 27, 2019, https://1ref.us/129.

156 Author unknown.

157 Antony, Saji, ed. "65. The Grocery Store." *40 Stories that Stir and Inspire*. Mumbai, India: Better Yourself Books/The Bombay Saint Paul Society, pp. 96–97.

158 Heck, Charles. "Love Is Patient." Worldly Saints: Seizing Life for the Glory of God. November 4, 2015. Accessed August 28, 2019, https://1ref.us/12a.

159 Conniff, Richard. "Race, Sex, and the Trials of a Young Explorer." Opinionator. February 13, 2011. Accessed August 28, 2019, https://1ref.us/12b.

160 MacDonald, William. "The Righteous Life Style Exalted." *Believer's Bible Commentary, Ebook, Second Edition*. Nashville, TN: Thomas Nelson, 2016, pp. 762–763.

161 Farcht, Joe. "How Good Is Life?" *Building Personal Leadership: Inspirational Tools and Techniques for Work and Life*. New York: NY: Genesis Publishing, 2007, pp. 211–212.

162 Kaminski, Debbie. Goodbye Past…Hello Purpose. "Apples and Kindness." May 20, 2019. Accessed August 28, 2019, https://1ref.us/12c.

163 Stanley, Charles. "How to Stay Young Your Whole Life." Encore on Blogs, April 2, 2009. Accessed August 28, 2019, https://1ref.us/12d.

164 Schuller, Robert H. "Journey for Life." Accessed August 28, 2019, https://1ref.us/12e.

165 "JetBlue Flight 292." Wikipedia. April 27, 2019. Accessed August 28, 2019, https://1ref.us/12f.

166 "Mother Teresa > Quotes > Quotable Quote." Goodreads, Inc. 2019. Accessed August 28, 2019, https://1ref.us/12g.

167 Brock, Robert W., Jr. *The Silent Church*. Maitland, FL: Xulon Press, 2009, 95–96.

168 Fisher, Marc. "Stark Prayer Sparks an Absolute Political Furor." *The Washington Post*. May 20, 1996. Accessed August 28, 2019, https://1ref.us/12h.

169 [Unknown]. 178. Horseman—Inspirational. Accessed, October 22, 2019, https://1ref.us/12i.

170 Davis, Margaret R. "November 3: Lip Service or Heartfelt Service?" *Fear Not!: Is There Anything Too Hard for God?* Fort Oglethorpe, GA: TEACH Services, Inc., 2011, p. 314.

171 "The Buried Life." October 17, 2012. Accessed August 28, 2019, https://1ref.us/12j.

172 Kersey, Donna. "The Pencil Story." God's Other Ways. 2015–2019. Accessed August 28, 2019, https://1ref.us/12k.

173 Stevens, Sherlene. *The Script in My Box: A Journey of Forgiveness*. "A Challenge." [From Stockdale, Allan A. Beyond the Gate (1983)]. Mustang, OK: Tate Publishing & Enterprises, LLC, 2012, p. 329.

174 "Rick Warren > Quotes > Quotable Quote." Goodreads, Inc. 2019. Accessed August 28, 2019, https://1ref.us/12l.

175 "Barack Obama Elected as America's First Black President." History.com. August 29, 2012. Accessed August 28, 2019, https://1ref.us/12m.

176 "The Gold Wrapped Gift," Stories of Kindness from Around the World. KindSpring. February 12, 2012. Accessed, October 23, 2019, https://1ref.us/12n.

177 "Secrets of a Happy Life." Happylife, December 4, 2008. Accessed August 28, 2019, https://1ref.us/12o.

178 Tolstoy, Leo. *Where Love Is, There God Is Also*. Springfield, OH: Crowell -Collier Company, 1885.

179 [Unknown]. "Help Us Remember." Prayer. Beliefnet. Accessed, October 23, 2019, https://1ref.us/12p.

180 Krogh, Steve. *Topography: A Pastor's Reflections on the Terrain Between Sundays*. Bloomington, IN: WestBow Press, 2019.

181 Luther, Martin. *Table Talk*. Gainesville, FL: Bridge Logos Foundation, 2004, p. 54.

182 Nikoley, Hans A. *My Daily Walk*. Maitland, FL: Xulon Press, 2006, p. 13.

183 Fillmore, Fred A. *Heart Songs for Sunday Schools*. Fillmore Brothers Publishers, 1893, p. 78.

184 "And God Said If...A Poem on Why God Allows Suffering & Trials." Next Generation for Christ, July 18, 2015. Accessed August 29, 2019, https://1ref.us/12q.

185 Landers, Ann. "Everyday Thanksgiving." *The Washington Post*, November 25, 1999. Accessed August 29, 2019, https://1ref.us/12s.

186 Author unknown.

187 "Happiness Is a Journey." Awakin.org. Accessed August 29, 2019, https://1ref.us/12t.

188 Muchiri, Mary Nyambura. "The Alphabet." *His Banner over Me Is Love: The Dreams of an African Woman*. Bloomington, IN: AuthorHouse, 2006, p. 215.

189 Faust, Jessica, and Sach, Jacky. "The Pilgrims Came." *The Book of Thanksgiving: Stories, Poems, and Recipes for Sharing One of America's Greatest Holidays*. New York, NY: Citadel Press, 2002, p. 23.

190 "The Only Survivor of a Shipwreck." Sermon Central. September 19, 2001. Accessed August 29, 2019, https://1ref.us/12u.

191 Mikkelson, David. "The Ant and the Contact Lens." Snopes. August 22, 2005. Accessed August 29, 2019https://1ref.us/12v.

192 Sherrick, Patricia A. "February 25, 2008" *Come Look with Me Through the Eyes of a Child*. Bloomington, IN: Xlibris Corporation, 2010, p. 174.

193 Smalley, Gary, and Trent, John T. *A Dad's Blessing*. Nashville, TN: Thomas Nelson, 1994, p. 9.

194 "John C. Maxwell > Quotes > Quotable Quote." Goodreads, Inc. 2019. Accessed August 29, 2019.

195 Jeremiah 35-1-19. "A Faithful Few." Accessed August 29, 2019, https://1ref.us/12w.

196 "Christmas is a Time—for Sharing." MumNatural. December 15, 2015. Accessed August 29, 2019, https://1ref.us/12x.

197 "The Colors of Christmas." Be Still Know That I Am God Judity316. December 21, 2013. Accessed August 29, 2019, https://1ref.us/12y.

198 "I'll Be Home for Christmas." Copyright Gannon & Kent Music, Co., Carlin America, Inc., Sony/ATV Music Publishing, LLC. Wikipedia. Accessed August 29, 2019, https://1ref.us/12z.

199 Morgan, Robert J. *He Shall Be Called: 150 Name of Jesus and What They Mean to You*. New York: NY: Warner Books, Inc., 2005.

200 DeHaan, M. R. "Can This Be Christmas?" Bible.org. 2019. Accessed August 30, 2019, https://1ref.us/130.

201 Barnett, Ralph. "Presence of Jesus at CHRISTmas." *Spiritual E-Soup: A Compilation of Inspirational Messages from the Internet*. Charlottesville, VA: E-Soup Ministry, 2007, p. 98.

202 Swindoll, Charles R. *Growing Strong in the Seasons of Life*. Grand Rapids, MI: Zondervan, 1983, 1994.

203 Clark, Willo Lou. "When Changes Come By." SermonCentral. February 14, 2001. Accessed August 30, 2019, https://1ref.us/131.

204 Waterman, Daniel. "Christmas Quotes." Faithlife Sermons. 2019. Accessed August 30, 2019, https://1ref.us/132.

205 Plewman, Cathy J. "When We Share." *Making Your Mind UP!: Thinking Skills for Grades 2–8*. New Haven, CT: Valley View Publishing Co., 2013.

206 Graham, John. "Concept of God." *The Foundation and Focus for Living: A Doctrinal Study of Scripture*. Bloomington, IN: Xlibris Corporation, 2009.

207 Capen, Richard G., Jr. "God's Gifts for Family and Friends." *Empowered by Faith*. Grand Rapids, MI: Zondervan, 2009, p. 156.

208 Smith, Gary W. "Christmas Poem." *Life Changing Thoughts: Thousands of Inspiring, Life-Changing, and Humorous Thoughts*. Bloomington, IN: AuthorHouse, 2009, p. 98.

209 Hudson, Josefina U. *Beautiful Words of Life*. Bloomington, IN: Xlibris Corporation, 2008, p. 158.

210 Ibid.

211 Sabbathi, P. I. "Why Jesus?" *Soulzer: Be a Spiritual Soldier to Undergird Your Own Soul*. Grand Rapids, MI: WestBow Press, 2014, pp. 33–34.

212 May, Steve. "A Lively Church." *The Story File: 1001 Contemporary Illustrations for Speakers, Writers, and Preachers*. Peabody, MA: Hendrickson Publishers, 2000, p. 4.

213 White, Ellen G. *Steps to Christ*. Mountain View, CA: Pacific Press Publishing Association, 1892, 70.1.

214 Smith, Gary W. "Wasted Years." *Life Changing Thoughts: Thousands of Inspiring, Life-Changing, and Humorous Thoughts*. Bloomington, IN: AuthorHouse, 2009, p. 635.

215 "Does God Expect Loyalty and Reliability?" Family Times. 2019. Accessed August 30, 2019, https://1ref.us/133.

216 Tucker, Larry A. PhD, and Bagwell, Marilyn, PhD. "Television Viewing and Obesity in Adult Females." *Am J Public Health*, 1991; 81:908–911. Accessed August 31, 2019, https://1ref.us/134.

217 "Sobering Questions for Church Members." *The Sabbath Sentinel*, July 1990, p. 12. From: *The Jerusalem Sentinel*, Fall 1989. Accessed August 31, 2019, https://1ref.us/135.

218 "Jonathan Edwards (1703–1758)." Bible.org. 2019. Accessed August 31, 2019, https://1ref.us/136.

TEACH Services, Inc.
P U B L I S H I N G

We invite you to view the complete
selection of titles we publish at:
www.TEACHServices.com

We encourage you to write us
with your thoughts about this,
or any other book we publish at:
info@TEACHServices.com

TEACH Services' titles may be purchased in
bulk quantities for educational, fund-raising,
business, or promotional use.
bulksales@TEACHServices.com

Finally, if you are interested in seeing
your own book in print, please contact us at:
publishing@TEACHServices.com
We are happy to review your manuscript at no charge.

www.ingramcontent.com/pod-product-compliance
Lightning Source LLC
Chambersburg PA
CBHW071656160426
43195CB00012B/1487